My Guyana

Stories of Growing Up in Guyana 1960-1977

Manorma Persaud

Copyright © 2024 MANORMA PERSAUD All rights reserved

The characters and events portrayed in this book are based on real events and people. Names have been changed to protect the privacy of characters.

No part of this book may be reproduced, or stored in a retrieval system, or transmitted in any form or by any means, electronic, mechanical, photocopying, recording, or otherwise, without express written permission of the publisher.

ISBN: 979-8320824376

Cover design by: KDP

Library of Congress Control Number: 2018675309

Printed in the United States of America

Dedication

To my beloved daughters, Nirvana, Karuna and Sarvani,
and my cherished granddaughter Calais

Introduction

This work tells my story which is based chiefly on my memories, but is also supported by the recollections of my family who were present before I was born, and of those who shared my life and experiences as we grew up together. I have no reason to doubt the veracity of information that was shared with me, for the stories from varied sources about my life before I developed memories of my own, do not differ.

I have often been asked by puzzled non-native Guyanese about how a person of East Indian descent, who had never been in India but who observes many Indian traditions, ended up in Guyana. Often Guyana is mistaken for Ghana, so I am careful to note South America when I give my country of origin. The explanation is simple; once slavery was abolished, workers were needed to keep the sugar plantations in Guyana, and elsewhere in the Caribbean, running. In this respect, our history is similar to that of the East Indians in other West Indian islands, especially Trinidad. The British (we were British Guiana before independence in May 1966), tried to use laborers from Portugal and China, but East Indians were more tolerant of the climate so mass importation of Indians ensued.

Workers were lured to leave their homeland, India, and undertake the journey to Guyana by false promises of easy work and easy accumulation of wealth in just a few years, in a place that was not far away. The recruits had no concept of the great distance they had to travel, across two oceans, until they were well on their way west. These new workers were indentured laborers which meant that they were paid for their work but had to provide their own lodging, food, and other necessities, during the period of indentureship. After their contract ended, the workers were free to return to India or live independently in Guyana. Many chose to stay since the meager wages they received did not allow for saving up enough to cover their and their family's passage back to the motherland. The Indians established roots and thrived. Most continued to work in the sugar estates at first, but segued into other professions over time. Guyanese of East Indian descent comprise over half the population of Guyana.

The first part of my story is set in Skeldon, now Corriverton, the hometown of my father and the town of my birth. Skeldon was, and still is, a bustling town on the Corentyne River. As was Indian tradition then, my grandfather's sons brought their wives to live in the family home after marriage, and so my uncle and his family, and ours, lived in the same home as my Aja, my grandfather on my father's side.

Our house was flanked by two clothing stores, and to the side of one of the stores, stood Palladium Cinema. There was a grocery store across the street, as well as Bovill's Pharmacy. The pharmacy boasted dark walls and shelves lined with bottles of powders and tinctures. Dr. Dean's Dental Practice was close to the pharmacy. A little further on was Mr. Wong Yeow's Dry Goods Store which sold everything imaginable, from pickled herring that sat in great wooden barrels, to colorful sweeties (our term for candy) to sewing thread. There was a lot for kids to do especially if they had a few pennies. Blacks and Indians comprised the majority of residents in Skeldon. There was also a smattering of Chinese, Portuguese, and a number of mixed-race families. There were no distinct neighborhoods for all races lived together in the same community.

In contrast to Skeldon, Orealla was a homogenous society of Amerindians. The two tribes there, the Arawak and Warrau shared a similar culture which became more alike and grounded after generations of living together in harmony. There was but a handful of outsiders who served mainly as teachers, government officials, and as part of the health care team. An offer of a position as headmaster of the elementary school, the only school in the village, brought my brother-in-law and his family to Orealla.

Living in Orealla was a unique experience for us; not only were we now immersed in a different culture, but the types of food we were accustomed to having were unavailable, as well as the conveniences of electricity, running water, cinemas, and shopping venues.

Port Mourant, located next to Rose Hall on the attached map from the Nation's Online Project, was Brother Edward's hometown. Like Orealla, it was also a homogenous society, but of East Indians rather than Amerindians. There was but a handful of people of other descent living there. Our family had the privilege of living in a home formerly owned by the British administrators of the local sugar estate; this meant indoor plumbing. The huge outdoor market allowed daily access to a wide variety of fresh foodstuff and treats. The small town of Port Mourant is well known in the cricketing world for being the birthplace of world-renowned cricket giants, among them are Rohan Kanhai, Basil Butcher, Joe Solomon, and Alvin Kallicharran, among others, who played on the West Indies Cricket team. Port Mourant is also the town where the former president of Guyana, Dr. Cheddi Jagan, was born and raised and educated in R. N. Persaud's small secondary school, the first in the area.

Each of these communities has changed drastically from the time I lived in them. They have become more westernized. Things we knew of only from movies or books before we moved abroad are now commonplace; television, cell phones, and the Internet have brought the rest of the world closer, and with it the ability to easily imitate what is considered desirable instead of being compelled to follow long-established traditions. Cultural norms have changed, the manner of dress, speech, food and behavior are different from what we experienced in the 1960s and 1970s. Old traditions do not hold sway anymore, and the creolese dialect we spoke may soon be obsolete.

I began writing this memoir so that my children could better understand the life I lived in Guyana during my childhood and youth. It is inevitable that many of the traditions and practices that were central to our lives then will disappear with the wave of change.

Chapter 1
My Fate is Decided

The women gathered under the pretense of bringing well wishes to the mother and her new-born child; mother and child lay cuddled in the jute hammock under the house. But that was the last thing on the women's minds right then. More than anything, they wanted to see if the baby had white blood. They were suspicious of a woman who was already a grandmother having a baby. And who can blame them? It was the kind of thing women took great pains to avoid after a certain age. But, they thought, Chachi worked in the gardens of the sugar estate residential compound and her master was a white manager from England, like all the managers were at that time. Mostly it was the young girls that caught the attention of the masters, but a drunk one, maybe he doesn't care about young or old or pretty or otherwise, maybe he would force himself on the nearest woman. And they all knew how this master, especially, liked his rum.

The gasps from those who faced the baby prompted the others to push their way forward to see what the gasping and covering of mouths was all about. It may or may not have registered that though the baby, a girl, was of a lighter complexion, she was not light enough to be carrying white blood in her veins. What grabbed their attention now was the blue-black stain that covered half the baby's face.

Normally, a light complexion would be much desired in a girl but in this case that was not going to do that girl one bit of good. If it was a boy, it might not have been so bad, but a girl? Who would marry her? Which family would want to tie bundle with a girl who was born cursed? They gathered onion and garlic and burned them over a fire and circled the child with the pungent smoke hoping to ward off the evil that came with her and make her pure.

Speculation as to the cause of the birthmark ran rampant. Maybe this child was beautiful but arrogant in a past life, or maybe she had disfigured another out of spite, and now karma was catching up with her, so she had to suffer this imperfection in this present incarnation.

Others laid blame for the mark on the mother. The mother was forty-two, way past normal child birthing age, and she was already a grandmother. Everyone knew that children born to women who were that old always had something wrong with them, either physically or mentally. They wondered aloud, in the mother's presence, whether she had no shame making babies at that age. Some recalled that when she was pregnant with this child the mother, unlike the other pregnant women in the village, did nothing to protect herself from the ill portent that accompanied the lunar eclipse or *Garahan a lagge* as the event is called in Hindi. She dared to snub the Gods by not walking outside and praying as the eclipse ran its course. Now her child was paying the price of her affront.

They women eventually decided among themselves that the stain on the child's face may not be such a bad thing after all, at least not for her parents and siblings. Sure, she will never get married and have a husband to support her, but God sent her for another reason; her purpose for being born was to take care of her parents in their old age. She would learn to sew and make a living as a seamstress as she tended to her parents' needs, and her siblings would not have to worry about who would bear that responsibility.

Through it all the mother sat still and numb, saying nothing, doing nothing, just cradling her child.

And so, my fate was decided, my life was planned out, supposedly according to the will of God, on the day of my birth. And all because of the stain on my face.

But the universe had other plans for me. The birthmark did cause pain, but it presented opportunities that would not have been afforded me if I had had a beautifully unblemished face

Chapter 2
What's in a name?

My mother was sixteen when she married and had babies soon after. She was forty-two when I was born and she was then the mother of three children in their twenties, one who was ten, and grandmother of four. Undoubtedly, I was a surprise, and as I later learned, not a pleasant one at that. At least not for my mother.

I do not blame my mother for being embarrassed at having a child at such a late age. It was nothing personal, for any baby would have produced the same feelings. Mother must have been the butt of jokes or snide remarks, in addition to the suspicion that surrounded my parentage. Luckily my father had no doubts. First thing he did was to take charge of naming me.

My grandfather Jaipersaud, a respected pandit in Skeldon, plotted the position of the heavenly bodies at the time of my arrival on Earth and determined that the auspicious first syllable of my name should be Ma. The time and day are crucial to choosing the name of a newborn. Those who did not have clocks or any other way to tell and record time, would rush to a pandit's house as soon as a baby was born, even in the dead of night and through any kind of weather, to make sure that the correct syllable, as dictated by the heavens at the time of birth would be known. Aja made many suggestions of names starting with the syllable *ma* that had wonderful meanings; Maheshwari, an epithet of the goddess Durga, Mahajaya, extreme victory, Mahadevi, referring to the greatness of the goddess Parvati, and several others. The hope was that a child would embody the characteristics of the chosen name. My father nixed all those suggestions. He named me Manorma, meaning beautiful.

The original name is supposed to be spelled Manorama in Hindi, and there are a few theories as to why the second *a* was dropped in my case. My sister said it was because my father wanted to Anglicize my name somewhat, some said the registrant, who was an Englishman, spelled the name phonetically and my father did not notice, and some said my father may have been partying and when he came to the registrar's office his spelling was a bit compromised. My bet is that the registrant spelled the name phonetically without asking for confirmation, a habit that was not uncommon and has resulted in many family members having a surname with varying spellings. This did not cause a problem until families sponsored their relatives to emigrate to the US or other countries. Often a deed poll would be required to prove that the sponsor and those sponsored were indeed parents, offspring or siblings despite the inconsistencies in the spelling of their surname.

Whatever the reason for the current spelling, I am happy with my name.

In addition to having an auspicious name so carefully chosen, I needed to have a nickname also. This was almost as important as my given name for it provided a protective shield should anyone attempt to put a hex on me. The given name was powerful and if one should decide to harm me, they could only do so if they used my astrologically determined name on which to focus the evil forces.

Being given a nickname was true of most children of Hindu Indian heritage in Guyana and like me, the use of their real name did not settle well at first. This usually occurred on the first day of school when children would be confused as to why the teacher was calling them by a strange name. It would take a while for them to be able to answer to their given name. Part of the difficulty of getting comfortable with the auspicious names was that they were usually long in order to incorporate all the virtues the parents wished their child to have. Nicknames were short and sweet.

My cousins who lived in the same home chose Anita for my nickname, and I was called by many endearing variations of this. I answered to Nita, Neet, Neets, and Anita. I did not start to use Manorma officially until I was about ten, when it was time to register for the Common Entrance Examination which determined high school placement. (I was able to continue using Anita in elementary school until then because my brother-in-law was the headmaster and my sister taught there. I bet it was easier for them to remember *Anita* also.) Since the proper given name was required to register for the Common Entrance exam I had to learn to listen for, and answer to Manorma, at least in school. It seemed foreign to be addressed as Manorma, especially when I was still called Anita by everyone who knew me. It would be decades before I would fully embrace my given name.

Chapter 3
Fate Steps In

The women were wrong about me having to take care of my parents in their old age. Their reasoning was logical at the time, but fate stepped in.

I was months short of my third birthday when my mother died. Pneumonia they said. Decades later I came to question this but was told pneumonia was written as the cause of death on the Death Certificate.

There was no doubt that my father could not raise me by himself; he was from a generation of men that had no dealings with cooking, housework, or raising children. That was woman's work. Fortunately for me, my three teenage cousins, two girls and a boy Sister Pat, Sister Judy and Brother Karanand, and their mother, my chachi, helped my father with this undertaking after my mother's passing. They loved me and cared for me. The ladies tended to my needs at home, and Brother Karanand put a pillow on the bar of his bicycle and towed me to kindergarten every day. My father had realized that I would most likely need to take care of myself as an adult on account of my birthmark. In a culture of arranged marriages and superstition, and the bad omen associated with such a prominent mark, it sounded the death knell for my prospects of finding a husband to support me. Pa felt that a solid education would lead to either a teaching or nursing profession which would allow me to be independent and comfortable.

To that end my father used his modest teacher's salary to give me a head start by paying for my attendance at a private kindergarten in Skeldon. The school was run by nuns of The Church of England, and the student body there was comprised mostly of the children of the British expatriate administrators of the local sugar estate, and wealthier native Guyanese. I was the only pupil of modest means.

My father's plans for me died with the massive stroke that felled him early one morning. He leaned over to tie his shoelaces as he dressed for school, fell over, and died instantly. People said it was a stroke. No autopsy was done for this was not common practice when the cause of death seemed cut and dried. Neighbors and friends proclaimed the diagnosis and cause of death. I believe the general sentiment was, *they died naturally, is the reason really that important?*

I was not yet five then. As I heard, Pa had made his wishes known that should he face an early demise I should go to live with my sister, Sister Enid, brother-in-law, Brother Edward, and their family, who now lived in Orealla, an Amerindian village on the Corentyne River. Orealla was an eight-hour boat ride away from Skeldon.

The August holidays were coming up shortly and it was decided that I would finish off kindergarten, which was already paid for, spend the August break in Skeldon, then go live with my sister and her family in time to start school in September.

Sister Enid, being twenty-three years older than me, had married and left home and had had three children of her own before I was born, and two after. All boys. She had lived in a town far away, even before moving to Orealla, so I did not know her or her family well. At four years old I was petrified at having to leave everything and everyone that was familiar to me to go and live with strangers as I saw them then, in a strange far-away place. I need not have worried. My sister's sons became the five best brothers anyone could ever hope to have.

Years later, as an English assignment, I wrote the following poem on the passing of my parents.

Gone

I remember when Pa died.
I was four.
I can still see the school children
in their tidy uniforms,
khaki shorts, blue shifts, white shirts,
standing at attention in perfect lines
in front of our house,
as they carried his coffin through.
I do not remember when my mother died.
I was two.
I have heard tell
that she loved to sing
and had taught my little cousin and me
to clap along as she sang.
I have heard tell
that when the ladies began to sing
her funeral songs,
my little cousin and I
laughed with glee and began
to clap along as they sang.

    I do not know what my mother looked like. There is no photograph of her. I do, however, have a clear image in my mind of a woman that I believe is my mother. When I describe the image to others, they without fail, say that is exactly what my mother looked like. Is it a memory, a dream, or something else? I cannot tell.

    There is one surviving photograph of my father. It was taken a few weeks before his passing for school purposes. According to those who knew him, he was ill then so the photo does not clearly reflect the person he was in real life.

Chapter 4
Pagli

Every time I hear the parable of The Widow's Mite, I remember Pagli.

Pagli is not her real name; Pagli means "mad woman" in Hindi, and it was the name given her by her husband, one of the town drunks. As I heard it, he chanted that word before blows, during blows, and after blows. The name stuck.

Pagli's parents had undoubtedly chosen an auspicious name for their child when she was born, a name that the heavenly bodies dictated, a name that would have held great meaning and would have been filled with hope and promise, but who could have foretold what the future held for her?

A back injury, most likely inflicted by her husband during one of his drunken rages, caused Pagli to walk with a pronounced stoop and she needed to use a walking stick. Her speech was slurred, maybe because of a blow to her face that damaged her mouth.

Everyone in town knew her story. Pagli had come to live in Skeldon from a far village after her arranged marriage. She had no relatives around and her husband prevented her from making friends and becoming close to anyone, a classic sign of an abuser as I later learned. She had sought shelter in my grandparents' home a few times before, when she was able to escape a beating. My grandfather was a respected pandit and his home was a safe haven for her.

A woman like Pagli had limited options to escape a bad marriage at that time and in that culture. She would not have been welcomed home by her parents for several reasons: it would have blighted the family name if their daughter left her husband, her sisters' chances for making good matches for marriage would suffer because of it, and the family was too poor to afford another mouth to feed. Working to have enough money to have a better life was out of the question for Pagli for her husband would never allow her to do so. So Pagli endured.

When he died, the townsfolk were happy for Pagli, but now she did not even have what little was left of her husband's paycheck after the rum shop. My grandparents offered her one of the rooms that the seasonal field hands would use, and she had whatever food was prepared, so Pagli came to live with us.

Pagli loved me.

Even though her needs for material things were covered Pagli insisted on begging. Whether it was to gain some sense of independence I do not know, but every day around noon, when folks would be on their way to the matinee show at the cinema, Pagli took her place by the roadside in the hot noonday sun. She would sit on her haunches, hands outstretched, right palm nestled in the left, waiting for the coins to drop. Her eyes remained downcast, whether in supplication or whether to avoid the pitying looks, only Pagli could say. Some gave and some crossed the road to avoid giving.

Pagli's take was never much, but whatever it was, at the end of each day she would seek me out from among the other children, take my hand and press her shiniest copper coin into my palm, close my fingers around it and hold my hand with both of hers for longer than necessary. I was about four then; a cent meant that I was rich, a penny (two-cent piece) put me in the luxury bracket. I spent Pagli's gifts on sweets at the shop under the house.

In later years, when I considered Pagli's actions I first thought that she showed me kindness out of pity, that she felt sorry for me after "my mother had died and left me" as it was phrased. This may have been partially true, but I came to believe that Pagli saw that I would be subject to the same evils that she suffered. The neighborhood children taunted "the beggar woman" because of her pronounced stoop and unsteady gait and her slurred speech. She knew that I would suffer similar taunts because of the birthmark on my face, but that I would be subjected to them earlier, as a vulnerable child. Being ridiculed because of one's physical appearance was an experience that not many shared, so Pagli could fathom what lay in store for me as no one else could. She showered me with attention and made me believe that I was special, and worthy, and loved, to cushion what lay ahead.

The more profound meaning of Pagli's kindness towards me was also lost on me as a child. I did not then understand the power of touch, of human contact, of having someone look into your eyes with a smile of unbridled joy and love, and unfettered gratitude because of something you did. Even if that someone was four years old.

Begging gave Pagli a coin and giving that coin, and witnessing the reaction it produced, reassured her that the horrors that had broken her body did not break her spirit. It helped her reaffirm that she still maintained the capacity to love and to receive love, to empathize with others, to be selfless and generous, to spread happiness, and to be human.

I wish I could tell Pagli that the Universe was good to the little girl that she loved, and who loved her. I want her to know that I survived the taunts and whatever ills came my way, and that I now live a happy, independent life.

I want to tell her that I wish I knew her given name.

I have a feeling that she already knows.

Chapter 5
Aja

My Aja was a respected and well-known pandit, or Hindu priest, in Skeldon. Aja's full-time occupation was that of head book keeper at Skeldon Estate, a job which few non-whites tended to be hired for. Such positions were usually the domain of the British expatriates, but Aja's proficiency with numbers served him well in obtaining this post. Aja observed the tradition of having his sons and their families move into the paternal home. This was a great arrangement for us children for there never was a shortage of playmates.

When Aja's original home became crowded, he sought to build an extension but the giant, iron water tank that stood next to the house did not make a seamless addition possible. The solution was to build an entirely new home in front of the water tank and close to the street. The two buildings, old house and new house as we all came to call them, were connected by a wooden bridge. The level of the doorways that the bridge spanned were not aligned perfectly so there was a slight downward slope from new house to old house. The bridge was the perfect place for us children to play when the adults needed their peace and quiet indoors.

Some of the extended family lived upstairs in old house. The downstairs had small rooms where field hands stayed during rice planting and processing seasons for Aja owned several acres of rice fields. One of those rooms was occupied by Pagli. I vaguely remember another woman who lived there, Auntie Sitajo. Auntie Sitajo was especially known for her earth-shattering belches, most of which were brought on by her penchant for cooking and eating spicy foods late at night. After she indulged, everyone expected the rest of the night to be punctuated by her gassy eructations, and Auntie Sitajo delivered without fail

One feature of Aja's house that impressed me the most was the grandfather clock that stood in the living room of new house. It had Roman numerals on a gold background and a hypnotic pendulum that swayed at a level with my eyes. The clock was an enigma to most of us. For a long while only Aja and his adult sons could read it, and later, his grandsons. Aja was the only one to open the door of the clock, clean it and wind it up when needed.

As I heard tell, my grandmother had no need for clocks. Ajee told time by the sun and the shadows it cast. When the shadow of the roof hit certain spots or objects, she knew what time it was. Since Guyana lies so close to the equator the position of the sun does not vary much so Ajee's method of telling time worked well, except on cloudy days, and *that* one time. Part of family lore reveals the one time that Ajee missed the mark by a long shot. It could have been because of an errant rooster who decided to give crowing a whirl at an unseemly hour. Ajee woke up the daughters-in-law to prepare meals for the field hands, both breakfast and lunch. The ladies worked with their usual efficiency and soon the meals were ready. Then they waited for the light of day. They waited and waited. Some nodded off. Finally, daybreak made its appearance, and the incident made its way into family lore.

Aja was a vegetarian. The only animal product he consumed was milk. His meals were prepared in cookware that had never held meat or eggs, and his food was dished out and brought to the table upstairs in new house. Aja never began eating without first taking a little of whatever he was served and putting it to one side of his plate. This was an offering of thanks to the Supreme Being offered before the meal was touched, and it was left uneaten. If the cat came around, and it usually did, Aja would make sure to place food for it from his plate.

The meals prepared for Aja were balanced; there was usually rice or roti, dhal, dahee (plain yogurt), cooked vegetables, and achar, a spicy and sour condiment. Meals were served with water or milk, and for dessert there was fresh fruit from the variety and abundance of fruit trees in the large garden at the back of old house.

One quirky habit that Aja had was to close all the windows of the house in the evening regardless of how hot it was. He had a belief that the night air was not good for one's health and everyone in the house knew and respected this. At least in new house where Aja lived. There was more freedom to have the windows open in old house. Another quirky habit that Aja had was the form of punishment he preferred to use. This was the twisting of one's ear with a firm grasp that hurt. I suppose it was his way of saying, "listen to me when I give instructions".

These two habits did not bode well for the young man of Chinese descent, one of my brothers' friends, who spent the night sleeping on the living room floor of new house. My brothers must have forgotten to tell him the rules laid down by Aja. Thus, this young man, to his detriment, opened a window in the night to let the breeze in.

Aja woke up later, felt the breeze and shut the window, but before returning to bed he gave the sleeping young man's ear a good, solid twitch. A kanaite, as it is known in the local language. Aja must have thought it was an errant grandson; it must have been difficult to tell in the dark. The young man must have thought it was a ghost, or who knows what, for he fled and was nowhere to be seen the next morning.

Chapter 6
Leaving Skeldon

I left the only home and family I knew, kicking and screaming. My grandfather, parents, my youngest brother, my cousins, and my widowed aunt, and Pagli, were all my family for nearly five years. My underage brother went to live with our eldest brother and family, Brother Maywah and Sister Marge and their four children, who lived nearby, after our parents died, and I was going to be with Sister Enid and Brother Edward and family.

Some said that I must have felt that a drastic change was before me to explain the unusual behaviors that I suddenly developed, habits that I did not display before. I began to scratch my head vigorously, with both hands, when anyone unfamiliar spoke to me, and I would not answer. I also began to have accidents that did not happen since I had been fully potty trained.

I can remember being picked up, flailing and bawling, as I was being carried away to depart for my new home.

Chapter 7
This Place called Orealla

It was August of 1961 when I came to live in Orealla, a few months before my fifth birthday. Brother Edward was headmaster of the Anglican mission school, and he, Sister Enid, and their five sons, Paschal, Remi, Roy, Dicky, and Joshua had moved to the village a year before I joined the family. We left Orealla in 1966 when Brother Edward's tenure there ended, and he secured a new position at a school on the coast.

I was riddled with trepidation at the new life that lay before me, but I need not have feared. I could not have known it yet, but I was about to embark upon the most exciting and adventurous years of my life in a setting that was rife with danger and yet harbored unparalleled, unspoiled beauty. Living in this village would also expose me to a culture unlike what I had known before, and the rich experiences offered by this environment could not have been replicated in any other place.

Orealla is a village of indigenous Amerindians situated on the western bank of the Corentyne River in Guyana. Guyana sits on the northern coast of South America. Prior to gaining independence in 1966 Guyana was under British colonial rule and was called British Guiana.

Two primary tribes, Arawak and Warrau, are the main inhabitants of Orealla. The long stretch of flatland that borders the riverbank is occupied chiefly by the Arawak while the two hills, one sandy and one composed of white chalk, are home to the Warrau. The word Orealla means "white chalk" in the Arawak language*1, and the gleam of the white cliffs when coming up the river from the coast is a welcome sight.

There were few non-Amerindians living in Orealla when we lived there. Our family, the district officer and his family, and the medical team, consisting of a nurse and her assistant were the only non-native full-time residents. A medic visited intermittently and mainly served in an administrative capacity to oversee health care. The English priest and his wife, Father and Mistress Tatnall, came every few months from their main parish on the coast to supervise the religious education of the mission, and to perform ceremonies such as baptisms and weddings that the Amerindian catechist, Owah Moshe, who conducted services when the priest was away, was not qualified to do. The bishop of the diocese came as needed for the confirmation ceremony of new converts to Anglicanism.

In the only mixed-race family there, the mother was of Amerindian descent and the father was a Guyanese of Chinese ancestry. Mister Chu, and his wife and children, lived some distance away on their farmland on the outskirts of the village, but the children attended our school. The father would drop off and pick up the three children to and from school each day by boat.

The Amerindians have features that are similar to those of the mongoloid race. Jet-black straight hair and almond eyes are common characteristics among both the Arawak and Warrau. The rounded features of the Arawak contrast with the more angular look of the Warrau who also tend to be a shade darker. The complexion of the natives ranges from tanned olive to coffee brown.

Legend has it that Orealla was founded in 1918-1919 when a flu epidemic felled most of the population of a village called Epira some miles up the river. The inhabitants of Epira fled their village because they felt that the destruction of their community was caused by an evil spirit who had put a curse on the settlement. One group of those who left Epira disembarked earlier to form the village of Siparuta and the other, larger group paddled a few miles further down-river to found Orealla*2.

Although the legend paints a romantic picture of the creation of the village, Church literature suggests that Orealla might have been settled more than half a century earlier. The annals of the Anglican Church in Guyana mention a book, "The Apostle of the Indians in Guiana", describing the missionary life of Reverend W. H. Brett. It was published in 1887 and states that Orealla was founded in 1866 by Reverend Canon Veness. One statement reads "Five years later, when the Mission was fully established, Mr. Brett...wrote to Mr. Veness under date June 23, 1871:'The Arawâk and Acawoio versions have now arrived at the Depository ... and I have put up 100 copies for your Mission at Orealla. . .*3 His letter was referring to some translations into English of the two native languages cited.

Orealla, and similar missions in Guyana and elsewhere, were founded through the passion and drive of missionaries who willingly gave up the comfort of their lives in developed lands to preach the word of God in remote, unchartered areas of the world. They often brought their young families, and together they braved the dangers of their unfamiliar surroundings. Many perished, if not through disease, then through attacks by unwelcoming tribes. There is an account of one, Mr. Youd, who lost his home, children, and wife as he tried to establish a mission in another region of Guyana. His wife was reportedly poisoned by a local sorceress and later Mr. Youd died from poisoning as well. *3. The mistrust and fear of strangers who were different from anyone that the natives had encountered before in looks, language, dress, and habits, motivated many attacks. The attitude of Amerindians became more friendly with familiarity, and so decades later when we arrived in Orealla our difference and presence were unremarkable.

Even if it was not instrumental in the founding of Orealla, the devastating flu mentioned was most likely the Spanish flu pandemic of 1918-1919. Perhaps a deadly wave of a different malady, a not uncommon occurrence throughout history, had prompted the exodus from Epira, and the settlement of Orealla and Siparuta, at a time before 1866, that gave rise to the legend. It is ironic that I am writing these words just over a hundred years later during the next pandemic, this one brought on by the novel Corona virus, or COVID 19. Despite its isolation, then and now, Orealla, like the rest of the world, is also battling this viral attack.

The population of Orealla was about a thousand when we lived there. Logging and farming were, and still are, the major sources of income, and the coastal towns of Skeldon, Springlands, and Crabwood Creek provided ready markets for the produce and logs. Crabwood Creek, known for its sawmills, was the anchor of the logging industry in that region.

The Amerindian diet then consisted of foods that remained unchanged for generations. Food supplies came directly from the land and river; cassava, other ground provisions, wild meat, birds, and fish were staples. Fruit grew wild and was abundant. Anyone could pick star-apples, mangoes, cashews, bilimbi, and guavas, among others. The only fruits one had to buy were those that were cultivated in farms, such as pineapples, which were simply called pine, watermelon, and bananas.

The one general store, owned and operated by Mr. Julius, filled the need for supplies that the villagers could not easily source from the environment. It stocked mainly essentials such as school supplies, batteries, matches, lamps, kerosene, fishhooks, and catgut for the fishing lines. Bolts of colorful cloth provided material for clothing which were sewn by local seamstresses. Ready-made clothing was not widely available anywhere in Guyana in those days. That came later in the 1970s, starting with the availability of Buffalo brand jeans. A few treats, including imported canned foods, soft drinks, and sweets were also available.

Mr. Julius' shop served as the local hangout spot for men to sit and discuss politics and business and other such weighty subjects over a beer.

What the mission offered far outweighed what it lacked. The adults in our family may have a different opinion of our time in Orealla for they had to worry about the health and safety of six children, but it was a place of marvel and adventure for us children. The years I spent in Orealla are, without a doubt, the most memorable of my childhood.

Chapter 8
Then Came Dawn

That first night in Orealla was not an easy one. We arrived late in the day, and amid the chaos of unpacking several months of supplies, and cleaning and preparing dinner, there was little time for anyone to explain the workings of my new surroundings to me. Roy, who was closest to my age, became my buddy but with the strangeness of everything, from people to surroundings, and being shy, I still felt lost. I picked at the plate of fried corned mutton and rice before me. At any other time, I would have relished this meal since canned goods were imported and thus expensive, so meals from cans were enjoyed as occasional treats.

That night I woke up needing to use the bathroom. I knew where the outhouse was, but it was some distance from the house and the night was pitch black. Electricity had not yet come to Orealla (that happened in 2007), all the lamps had been turned off for the night, and the moon was hiding.

I looked under the beds for a chamber pot, or posey as we called it, like I was accustomed to using at night in Skeldon but did not see one. After all, boys do not need chamber pots, a clear, discreet spot outdoors would do just fine. I approached the kitchen door several times and undid the latch, but fear held me back from stepping outdoors. The night noises here were strange and unsettling, accustomed as I was to the city sounds of Skeldon. The toots of car horns, music and dialogue that escaped from the open windows of the nearby cinema, and the chorus of drunks after the rum shops closed, were comforting in their familiarity. Here the shrieks of night birds, the guttural croaking of bull frogs and at times, the complete, pregnant, silence were unnerving that first night.

I paced the hallway and considered waking up someone to accompany me outside, but I could not muster up the courage to do that since I barely knew anyone enough to impose upon them. After I could bear it no longer, I just succumbed and did what I needed to do. On the bedroom floor. It was not a voluntary act. The agony of a full bladder was replaced by cold and shame. In those days it got cold at night in the tropics, so I sat shivering by the bedpost in my wet nightgown with tears streaming down my face, wondering about the reactions I would receive in the morning when everyone found out what I had done.

Then dawn broke.

And what a sight dawn was! Since I was up before everyone else, I stood alone and watched the sun begin its graceful climb out of the far end of the river. The huge picture windows, without glass and with their canvas covers raised to let the breeze in, offered a stunning view of the east. A golden ribbon streamed along the dark, still, waters of the Corentyne, and the bamboo that graced its near banks was cast in lacy silhouette against the rising sun. The outlines of the forests on the opposite bank of the river, the Suriname side, created an irregular gray-black border that lined the edge of the brightening sky. The smell of fruit, too ripe and heavy to dangle from their stems any longer, now wafted up from the warming earth under the trees that they had fallen from during the night. Their fruity scent mingled with that of the morning glories that climbed the house post below the window, their faces turned towards the young sun.

I stood in awe as the unseen hands of the Artist blended the colors, pink and purple and peach, and gold and white, and blue in His ethereal pallet, and painted the morning. The symphony of a light breeze whispering through the bamboo, the lilting tunes of morning birds, and the growls of what I later learned were howler monkeys, urged the world to wake up and greet the day.

I could not have put it into words at that young age, but I knew then that all would be well.

Chapter 9
My New Home

My new home was light and bright. Whoever designed it created huge openings in the walls of the living area instead of standard sized windows. One offered a clear view of the stelling (the word stelling, of Dutch origin, is used in Guyana and the Caribbean as a synonym for a wharf) in the east, and two ran along the side of the house that faced the main footpath of the village that was separated from the river by a grove of bamboo. There were no shutters or glass on these openings. When shade or cover from rain was needed, sheets of canvas would be released from hooks at the top and rolled down. The wooden roller would be secured with the attached strings to large nails on the underside of the windowsill. Depending on the strength and direction of the wind during a storm, rain would often pelt into the house from the sides and bottom of the canvas sheets and soak the living areas of the house. Creases between the planks in the unvarnished wooden floor would drain most of the water away but we had to scramble to remove the hammock and books or games at the first signs of heavy rain.

In good weather the canvas sheets would be left rolled up to let in the river breezes, a practice that allowed me to behold that glorious view of my first morning in Orealla. An L-shaped wooden bench was built-in along the walls below the corner windows and a small wooden table sat in the L. This was chiefly the children's area. It was where we did schoolwork or reading when it was light outside or played cards or board games. In the evenings we sat on the floor of the dining room which was lit with the Tilley gas lamp and read. Brother Edward and Sister Enid usually did their paperwork for school on the dining table, where the lamp sat, after their evening chores were done.

What we called the gallery was my favorite spot. The most coveted seat in the house, at least among us children, was the hammock that hung from the gallery beams. It was not a traditional Amerindian cotton hammock, but one made of jute bags as was common in homes on the coast. The jute bags formerly held rice and were stitched together to fashion hammocks. At times flour sacks would be used to make a softer hammock but these sacks were more prized for bedsheets or coverlets. Bed linens made from flour sacks become very soft over time and are often prized over those made from other materials. The logo of my favorite flour sack coverlet faded over time but the faint imprint still lingered for many years.

The hammock became the source of many arguments as to whose turn it was to lie in it, and with good reason. Curling into a hammock that wraps around you primes one to become transported into another world with little other than a good book or a fertile imagination. This hammock was also the spot where our story tellers, Sister Enid and Uncle, sat as they spun fanciful tales to the rapt audience squatting on the floor around them.

An indoor bathroom stood in a lean-to that extended from the dining room. Because of its strange location I suspect it was added sometime after the house proper was built. It was more convenient than trying to exit an outdoor bath house in a modest manner. This bathroom was meant for bathing and brushing teeth only. Other needs were served by the outhouse. The wooden floor had many wide creases where the water drained out onto the grass below and through which snakes could slither in or out of. Checking for snakes before entering the bathroom or outhouse was a routine that became second nature to us. There was no indoor plumbing. A tin tub, which we called a bakey, sat along one wall. We would carry water up the stairs from the rain barrels that stood at the foot of the kitchen stairs and fill the bakey for bathing. The water was always cold. Always. Brother Edward's method of dealing with the first bone-chilling splash was to make loud whooshing and gasping sounds as the water hit. A stranger might have thought he was being attacked. Maybe by a snake. A very aggressive snake. My method was to count to three then brace myself and splash. Some say it is invigorating to wash with cold water. I say it is brutal.

The outhouse stood some distance away from the main building, as outhouses generally are, and for good reason. Every now and then Jeyes fluid would be added to the pit and used to disinfect the wooden surfaces. Right after a treatment with this cleaner the outhouse smelled like a hospital which makes me believe that hospitals in Guyana used this product as a disinfectant.

Brother Edward made sure the grass around the latrine was always kept short. All the better to see lurking snakes, and to make the environment less inviting to them. Before we would arrive to the village after school breaks, word would be sent ahead by the regular boatmen so that church members would cut the grass around the outhouse and rid it of vermin if needed. Cutting the grass was done the old-fashioned way, with cutlasses, or machetes as some call them; no one then had ever heard of lawnmowers. The short grass deterred most, but not all, of the slithering menace so one still had to approach with caution when visiting the outhouse.

The bedrooms, with several beds to a room, all with mosquito nets and sparse furniture, adjoined the living room. Our everyday clothes were stored in cardboard boxes because of limited storage space. We collected the boxes from the large grocery stores on our stock-up trips to the coast. Each of us could tell which was our clothes box by what it had previously held. Mine was the Ovaltine one. I was glad I did not get the Horlicks box because I preferred Ovaltine over Horlicks. Fry's Cocoa was so-so. Whoever made cocoa never added enough sugar to make my tongue happy. I do not remember who got the box that once held Seven Seas Cod Liver Oil, but I sure was glad it was not me, I had too many unpleasant memories of that product. Our "good" clothes, as we called our Sunday best, were neatly pressed and folded and placed in a trunk under the bed. Our beds were of typical height for beds in Guyana then; there was no box spring so that allowed for tall objects to be stored underneath. Mothballs were added to protect the clothes and I have always associated the smell of mothballs with nice clothing.

The nets over the beds were draped over wooden hoops that hung from the rafters. They were supposed to keep out mosquitoes but whoever designed them failed to consider the exceptionally smart, innovative specimens throughout Guyana. We would check to make sure that there were no holes in the nets, or that there were no mosquitoes trapped in them before we went to sleep, but no matter how carefully we tucked the nets around the bed those critters managed to find a way in and feed on us all night. In the direct light of the morning sun, we could see our bright red blood shining through their transparent bodies. Our blood, now theirs, would smear our hands when we slapped them dead.

My sister created a kitchen that was a child's dream. It was not that she meant to fashion a unique, exciting, kitchen; she merely used her creativity to cover up the soot stains on the walls that were impossible to scrub off. Even though the kitchen extended away from the main frame of the home and had windows on three sides and a door, the soot from the wood-burning fireside still lingered on the walls and the stains stayed forever. In the absence of paint or wallpaper Sister Enid resorted to using the materials she had at hand. These were the old copies of magazines, mainly Women's Day, that she had saved after everyone had read them. She cut out the most colorful and interesting pages, the majority of which featured food, and pasted them on the walls with a flour-and-water mixture. When these became too sooty, they would be replaced with a new set.

We had never seen most, if any, of the foods pictured but we knew they had to be delicious for our senses told us so. There were chocolate cakes of several layers with icing in between, fruit pies, beef roasts with potatoes and carrots, trifle, and a host of other delicacies. There were even whole chickens, roasted in a pan and surrounded by colorful vegetables. We were familiar with chicken, but we had never seen one cooked whole. It was always chopped into smaller pieces and curried or stewed with vegetables and potatoes. I did not see many of the foods featured until decades later. In fact, if the ketchup or mayonnaise or other condiments that were in the ads were put before me while I was in Guyana, I would not have known what to do with them.

Mrs. Tatnall, the priest's wife, offered the best evaluation of the decor when she remarked to my sister "Oooohhh, Mrs.Mack, your kitchen makes me drool at all the delicious food before me." I can only imagine how this lovely lady must have hungered for those foods that she had enjoyed before in her native England, at least when she first came to Guyana. Now her diet mirrored the less varied, and mostly spicy meals we ate. Mrs. Tatnall began collecting and saving copies of women's magazines for my sister and brought them when she visited so there was never a shortage of replacement "wallpaper".

Our everyday plates were colorful, and none matched. They were made of enamel and each one had a different painted scene on it. I am glad that we never had a matched set because that would have robbed us of the excitement of choosing a favorite pattern. Only the "ware" plates, short for chinaware or dinnerware, that were reserved for company, all looked the same. The plate I cherished most had a picture of a red rooster with an impressive comb and a tail of brilliant green feathers. If roosters could be said to have an expression, I would describe his as cocky. I regretted letting on that this was my favorite plate for when Roy wanted to get back at me for something or the other, he would make sure to grab this one first and taunt me with it. Our plates, like the enamel cups, all had chips and dents but that did not diminish the beauty of my rooster plate.

The kitchen also provided a source of reading materials. New reading material was always available in the labels on cans and spice jars, or in the descriptions of foods on the walls. I learned that tartar sauce, whatever that was, was served with fish, and that what the magazines called stew, was vastly different from the stew we ate with rice. Reading and scrutinizing the pictures on the labels, with a lot of time to think about what I saw and read, led me to think deeply about the woman in the sari on the can of Chetty's curry powder. She held a can of the same curry powder, with a picture of the same woman holding the same can, and so it went. It occurred to me that if you could make pictures small enough that scene would never end. I did not know the word infinity then.

Chapter 10
The Three Rs

When I first moved to the village, Orealla Anglican Mission School taught classes in The Holy Epiphany Anglican Church that sat next door to our house. It was a primary school, Preparatory A through Fourth Standard. There was no higher education beyond this available in the village or nearby. Those who wanted to attend high school after Fourth Standard had to leave the village to further their studies in secondary schools on the coast. This meant writing and scoring well in the standardized Common Entrance Exam. Most students never sat this exam since leaving Orealla to attend school was not an option open to many. Often those who had access to the extended education returned to Orealla to teach.

The younger children, in Prep A and Prep B, sat in the front pews and wrote on slates while the higher classes in the back of the church used exercise books. The headmaster and teachers shared the vestibule to store their books and supplies. On Monday mornings the pews were rearranged from church seating to classroom format. There were no dividers except for chalkboards on easels. On Friday afternoons everything was moved, the church was swept clean, and the furniture was rearranged again for Sunday worship.

But this situation was about to end. A new primary school was being built by the government at the other end of the village in the area where the District Officer lived, and it was almost ready to hold classes. The church school had served the village well for many years, but it was now overcrowded so the government stepped in to build a larger one. The new school would be called Orealla Government Primary School.

The new structure had none of the charm and quaintness of the church building. It boasted an industrial look that was designed to be functional rather than aesthetically pleasing. The quaintness of the whitewashed shingles that layered the outer walls of the church was replaced by nondescript concrete walls. Where the interior of the church housed a raised altar section and had nooks and crannies and niches for floral arrangements, the new school was a plain, flat rectangle with no arresting details. White wooden shutters had graced the windows of the mission school, but the government school sported greenish glass louvered windows housed in metal slots. The comforting smells of incense and candlewax that mingled with those of the flowers from Sunday service, especially on Monday mornings, were gone. Now instead, the smell of concrete and paint intermingled with those of chalk dust and graphite.

The functional design of the new school, and the fact that it did not also double as a church gave us at least one great advantage besides classroom space; we now had space on the walls for posters that could stay up indefinitely. There was a plethora of maps, both political and topographical, diagrams of the parts of seeds and trees, different types of trees and the zones in which they grew, types of rocks, and many more, most with a scientific bent. There was now also room to celebrate the artwork of students by featuring them on the walls.

I had started out in Prep A in the church school, but since I had the advantage of attending kindergarten, an opportunity whom few had, my teacher had assessed that I already knew the material, so I was placed in Prep B in the new school for the rest of that year.

I was happy to be in Prep B. This was good in two ways; I was learning new material and I was in Miss Emma's class. Miss Emma was a native Amerindian. She was soft spoken and elegant; she always wore her hair up and her back was ramrod straight. Being placed in Prep A would have meant that Sister Enid would have been my teacher, and though I loved my sister, I was none too keen on being in her class. She proved to be a strict disciplinarian at home, and I was sure she would expect the same standards of behavior at school.

Sister Enid was recruited to teach Prep A since the expansion of the school resulted in a shortage of teachers and a high school education was all that was needed to teach professionally. This was true even when I finished high school more than a decade later. Many of my classmates and I assumed teaching positions right after passing enough subjects in the General Certificate of Education Ordinary Level exams. I can think of only two of my teachers throughout high school who had a bachelor's degree. The others were high school graduates, some of whom had formal training in teaching at the Teacher's Training College in Georgetown. This facility offered teaching certificates but not degrees. Whatever the education level of our teachers, their care and dedication earned them the respect of their students as they steered us on to success. Our parents and guardians were also instrumental in our academic achievements. Without their discipline at home and their steadfast support of our teachers' efforts, we may not have succeeded.

The new school was still a one-room schoolhouse with Prep A anchoring one end and Fourth Standard the other. A dedicated headmaster's office and staff room served the needs of the teachers.

Blackboards on easels doubled as classroom dividers in the absence of inner walls. The new blackboards were larger than those in the church, but privacy was still an issue. This was of especial disadvantage to me since Sister Enid, at an anchor end of the building had a clear view of the entire school. This meant she could see me wherever I was, and what I was doing. She saw how I struggled with sewing; my thread was always longer than I could easily manage, and I frequently had a knotted mess on my hands. It made me nervous when I saw her watching me, but I grew to like sewing anyway. I liked embroidery even though, to this day, I cannot do a blanket stitch.

The worst thing, however, was when Sister Enid signaled my teachers that I was talking. I tended to talk in class. A lot. Every punishment I have ever received as a student was related to talking. My sister must have thought this unusual since I did not speak much at home but at school, or with my friends, I chattered, or would *par-par* as it was called in the colloquial tongue, non-stop. The effect was that the teacher would either hit my palm with a ruler or my head with a book. They probably felt more obliged to punish me since my behavior was noticed by the headmaster's wife. Despite the efforts of Sister Enid and my teachers, this habit persisted throughout my schooldays.

I loved school and especially the "library" books we could take home. I use the term library very loosely. A collection of books was stored in boxes in the headmaster's office. On library days the assigned teacher would lay them out on a table and students would come up in groups to make their selection. The older students got first pick. If you had one that you borrowed on a previous library day, the teacher would make a note in his library exercise book that it was returned and then you could choose another.

If anyone in the United States, Canada, or the United Kingdom has ever wondered if the books they donate to missions have an impact on the children's lives there then I am living testimony that they do. At home we had a small selection of books that Brother Edward took great care to preserve. We could read them anytime we wished, in fact, we were often encouraged to "go read a book", but they were kept on a high shelf and covered with thick brown paper. We had to ask for them and it was understood that they would be handled with care. There were five treasured volumes, Grimm's, and Anderson's Fairy Tales, Aesop's Fables, Mother Goose Nursery Rhymes, and Illustrated Bible Stories for Children. They were large, hard-covered volumes with glossy pages, and we read them over and over. I especially loved the illustrations in some of the books, which I believe were done by Eric Kincaid; the little fairies and pixies that were hidden in the background were a thrill to find. We also had a few other books that we received as gifts from the priest and his wife when they visited. I remember a copy of Little Black Sambo which we enjoyed without an inkling of any deeper meaning that caused controversy in later years.

And so, the boxes of donated books from abroad fed our appetite for new reading material. Since Orealla had no electricity, and television was decades away from being introduced to Guyana, reading provided a glimpse into the lives of others in far-away places. One of my favorite books had chapters with titles such as, "A Day in the Life of a Bedouin Boy", or "A Day in the Life of an Eskimo Girl". I was not much concerned with the bigger picture in any of these stories, it was the minutia that fascinated me. What they had for breakfast, or where they slept, and the kind of home they lived in were of greater importance because their lives differed so much from ours.

Our only live contact with the world beyond on a regular basis was a Phillips radio powered by a huge blue Berec battery that sat alongside it. The words "BBC World Service, the news, read by…" let us know, every morning, that it was seven o'clock. Batteries were expensive, however, and the one used for the radio was not available in the village, so we needed to conserve what we had in case of emergency. The radio was a vital commodity and it sat in a protected corner on a high stand. Only Brother Edward and Sister Enid could turn it on or off; we were not allowed to touch it. News broadcasts were a staple and Sister Enid listened to Indian Music Hour on Sundays.

The one program that we all gathered around the radio for was the Sunday night presentation of Art Linkletter's "Kids say the Darndest Things" brought to us by Spiegel, Chicago's most famous mail-order house. I wondered why Mr. Spiegel had to order his house through the mail. And how it was delivered. And if there were a lot of these mail-order houses in Chicago, and why was Mr. Spiegel's the most famous one. It seemed to me it would have been much easier to just build a house where one wanted it to be. Our mail on the coast was delivered by a postman in a khaki outfit and a cork hat who rode a bicycle and carried the mail in a canvas sack. I wondered how mail was delivered in America to accommodate a house. I supposed that was one of those things I would understand when I got older.

I devoured the books I borrowed from school, and there was one I loved so much that I wanted to read it again. As I remember, it was called *The Five H Club*, but the teacher felt I should choose a higher-level book instead to further my reading skills. No one else in our group wanted to borrow that book but he refused to let me have it. I could not understand his decision and I never read whatever one it was that he handed me.

Chapter 11
Genesis

There was only one church in Orealla when we lived there, the Anglican Church, or the Church of England, as it is sometimes called. My recent research has shown that there are now several other Christian denominations in the village.

Since the mission church was established in 1866*3 Christianity became the main religion, effectively replacing any tribal religious observances that may have existed before. The population all bore Biblical or English names, both first names and surnames. The native language was all but obsolete and the traces of it that still lingered among the younger residents were songs and the words for traditional objects. Standard English was spoken in school and Church but only to teachers and those in authority; among friends and family the main language of communication was Creolese.

Creolese is spoken throughout Guyana. It is a form of English that features distorted pronunciations and the addition of words from the two major cultures, East Indian and African. Speakers of traditional English may not recognize it as being English at first.

The priest may not have easily understood Creolese, and his congregation in Orealla did not easily grasp the accent of a native Englishman, especially if he was delivering an impassioned sermon. Language did not present a barrier to attending church, however. Father Tatnall preached to a packed house whenever he visited and commanded greater attendance than Owah Moshe who spoke standard English in Church out of respect for the institution, but with an accent his audience could understand. He was also known to lapse into Creolese if he wanted an especially important nugget of wisdom to sink in.

We, the older children in the family, went to church every Sunday. The building was next door so there was no escaping it. The three of us, Remi, Roy, and I sat together in the front pew, and when Dicky was old enough to attend, he sat by his father in the back. Paschal had left Orealla to attend secondary school in New Amsterdam the year after I joined the family, but he would sit with us when he came back during school breaks. We chose the row to the right of the altar, to avoid the sprays of spittle that rained down on those in the front middle pews by enthusiastic preachers. Given the choice we would not have sat in such a conspicuous spot. We preferred the seats in the back where it would be less noticeable if we fidgeted or nodded off, but we were commanded to sit up front. Brother Edward kept a close eye on us from the back, especially after the time the three of us broke out into uncontrollable giggles. We heard the low "pooooooof" of a long, drawn-out fart. Others must have heard it too but they were either more mature or had greater self-discipline than we did. For three elementary school children, however, this was prime entertainment. At first, we chuckled quietly, but then we looked at each other and the giggles took over. Owah Moshe had to pause his sermon.

We may not have learned anything from Owah Moshe's sermon in church that day, but we learned plenty about respect from Sister Enid's sermon when we came home. We were told how disrespectful we were to Owah Moshe, the congregation, and to God, and how we ought to be ashamed of the way we acted, how we were "hard ears" and behaved as if we had no training. People would think that no one bothered to train us. Repeat. Repeat. Repeat. We realized that we were wrong, were remorseful and accepted the punishment, but my sister's words and their meaning became lost after the first repeat. We sat through the lecture without giving other cause for punishment.

Repeating that incident has become family lore over the years.

Sister Enid did not attend church that often since she had to prepare a big midday meal on Sundays. That took several hours. She mostly attended when the priest visited, and would then hire extra help to manage the chores. On the Sundays that my brother-in-law had a lot of work to catch up he too was absent but Remi, Roy, and I were the faithful attendees, though not by choice.

You could always tell when Brother Edward was not in church for the singing was noticeably subdued. We each had our own copy of The Book of Common Prayer which had traditional hymns along with Psalms, Prayers, and Creeds, but I noticed that Brother Edward rarely looked at his when he sang. I later learned that he could not read the very fine print in the Book, so he sang from memory. Trouble was, his memory for recalling hymns was not very good, and his singing voice had as much melody as needle across vinyl. He sang the verses he remembered loud and clear, and he also sang the ones he did not remember loud and clear; he just substituted his own words. If my sister happened to be present, she would give him the elbow even though it was not always effective. I have often wondered if this had anything to do with her not going often to church. Brother Edward's enthusiastic singing made us wince in the front pew, but I am sure he won points with God for his unbridled joy at singing songs of praise.

When we became old enough to help, we assisted with chores around the church. Roy and Dicky would ring the church bells every Sunday afternoon at five minutes to three to alert the children that Sunday school would soon be starting. I would gather flowers for the altar and help sort and put away prayer books.

Chapter 12
Spare Not the Rod

Sister Enid was the disciplinarian at home. She was very strict and had many rules that we needed to follow. When I grew older, I could better understand her need to be so demanding. It must have been nerve wracking to keep track of the whereabouts of six young children in a place where danger lurked everywhere, so she did her best to warn us to keep us safe. Sister Enid also wanted us to adopt the values and morals that she grew up with. The Amerindian lifestyle was more relaxed than that of an East Indian household and she wanted us to uphold Indian as well as Christian modes of behavior. Her chosen method of instilling these values was through lecturing. The length of her admonitions, and her propensity for repetition, are legendary.

Brother Edward proved to have a more subdued method of discipline. For minor transgressions he would wag his index finger and sternly reproach the boys with a "make it the last time, boy. Make it the laaaast time." He would only yell and grind his teeth in anger for major offences, but his tirades lasted for all of five minutes, unlike the days-long reproaches of my sister. Their disciplinary styles reminded me of what one neighbor, Auntie Rana, who years later, said of man rain and whooman rain. Man rain tended to be a heavy rainfall, maybe accompanied by thunder and lightning, but its duration was short, leaving room in the day for other activities. Whooman rain, on the other hand, was a slow drizzle that lasted all day long and sucked the joy out of the day with wet grayness.

The few times I observed Amerindian children being disciplined all it took was a sharp admonishment from the parent, usually a word or two, and the child would look remorseful, and that was that. I do not remember anyone apologizing for doing something wrong when I was a child, in either culture. There was no need to say "I'm sorry" for all that was expected was a look of remorse and respectful silence when punishment, mostly verbal, was meted out.

That is why it was surprising when four boys were caned before the entire school in Orealla on one occasion. The usual punishment for misbehaving in school was a few slaps in the palm with a ruler for girls, a light lash with a cane across the legs for boys, or a *thunk* at the back of the head with a book for anyone who was not paying attention.

On this occasion, however, the parents and staff privately discussed the appropriate punishment for the four boys, all students in the Fourth Standard. I do not know what they had done, it was one of those hush-hush topics that children were not privy to, and I did not even hear my sister and Delia talking about it. But we all knew it had to be something serious to warrant the public whipping they received.

On the appointed morning, the parents brought their sons to school. The area behind the Fourth Standard was cleared and a desk was set in the middle of the clearing. The pupils in Forth Standard were asked to turn around and face the desk so that everyone in the school could witness what was to happen.

One by one the boys were brought forward, asked if they knew why they were being punished, then they were directed to bend over the desk and were caned, six times each. Brother Edward carried out the caning. He pulled the shorts that the boys wore taut so that they could better feel the sting of the lash. Boys were known to wear several sets of underwear if they knew they were going to be caned and I hope those boys did.

Each boy cried, and so did their mothers, while the rest of the audience stared solemn-faced at the proceedings.

I think Brother Edward suffered as much as the boys for having to dole out such punishment.

I imagine that whatever the incident was, it involved the school or pupils. If it has been acts of vagrancy or any misbehavior that occurred outside of the school's jurisdiction it would have been brought before the village captain, a native Amerindian who was chosen by the villagers. Captain helped resolve disputes or gave advice, direction, or assistance as needed.

Chapter 13
Assembly

The government school had a large schoolyard and every morning we had assembly outdoors, unless it rained, then assembly would be skipped.

The classes would line up in order of rank and the pupils stood still while the teachers spoke. If you were caught talking to a friend or fidgeting, chances are that you would be called up in front to share what was so important. A student once stuck out her tongue at another and had to repeat the act before the audience. That helped me mind my behavior.

Being first in line was a goal many strived for. I was not one of those pupils. Standing behind someone who was taller and wider suited me just fine. It gave me the freedom to drift off during the announcements as I was wont to do, and to avoid being called on to answer any questions posed by the teachers. Sometimes there would be a trivia question, or one would be asked to repeat an important announcement that was just said to make sure you were listening. Students did not raise their hands in eagerness even if they knew the answer so the teachers would be forced to call on someone. There was not a single Hermione Granger (Harry Potter fans would understand) among us. Judging by how seldom I was called, being tiny was not such a bad thing.

We did not start assembly with prayer as we did in the church setting. First the news of the day and any announcements would be shared. If the entire school was practicing special songs for a concert or some sort of celebration, we would have a practice run during assembly. Then the physical exercise session would begin.

One of the teachers would preside over jumping jacks, breathing drills, where we would take a deep breath and hold it for a count to ten, balancing practice where we would stand on one leg and then the other during a countdown, and stretching exercises. These involved stretching our arms as far as we could per the instructions of "Up! Down! In! Out!" Then we would bend and touch our toes and would stay put through "Hold it! Hoooold it! Hooooooold it! Stand straight! Shake up!" And scores of bodies would wiggle in place.

These exercises were meant to energize us in preparation for the day ahead. Very few students needed that for many of us would come early so that we could get in a few schoolyard games, or a climbing session or two on the calabash tree before the bell rang.

Assembly ended with us singing a patriotic song before filing in neat lines to our classes.

Chapter 14
Our Neighbors

Errol and Tucko who lived next door, were about the same age as Roy and me and we ended up being best friends. We would often go over to their house to play, and if they had chores to finish, we would help them so that we could start our games quicker. My sister and Delia warned us not to wander far away from home. The dangers were many, snakes, the river with piranha, steep slopes, evil spirits, stinging insects, and a host of other terrors. Errol and Tucko's house could be seen from our house and so it was considered safe.

Their yard had everything to keep a child entertained for hours on end. There was the squat calabash tree with spreading branches that we would climb and then jump off on to the sandy floor below, then climb again and do it all over. We were careful not to break the gourds for Errol's father would remove the pulp and carve them to make bowls of various sizes, and goblets for storing drinking water. Glasses and chinaware were not part of the native dinnerware; bowls, cups, and spoons made of calabash served every dining purpose. Errol's dad took care of such tasks when he was at home in between hunting sessions outside of the village.

The huge star apple tree that stood in the middle of the yard bore the sweetest fruit, but they often harbored worms. Errol would just scoop out the worm and continue eating but Roy and I were too squeamish to follow suit. Antepar syrup, a thick, green anti-parasitic medicine was a fixture in our house, so Sister Enid was prepared just in case we did such things.

Part of the children's chores would be to clear up the overripe fallen fruit that lay squashed under the trees. We preferred the ones that were just ripe and when we pelted small rocks at those that grew on the higher branches to get them to fall, we would dislodge many leaves in the process. We were expected to help clean up the mess we made and we did so without question.

When the four of us had exhausted all the fun to be had down-the-hill we would head up the sandy hill behind the house and slide down on our home-made sleds. We made these from the boat-shaped "skin" parts that were shed from coconut trees. When dried these made a light, sturdy container for small bodies. Sledding the hill was an exhilarating but exhausting activity for we had to haul our sleds up the hill, slide down, and then start over. Since we had to maneuver the loose sand as we climbed our feet soon tired. What was worse was that we would get sand stuck in our hair and this was no easy task to wash out with a limited supply of water. Sister Enid or Delia would have to dip water from a bucket and then scrub with vigor for a good while to get all the sand out. Having to endure this process was enough of a deterrent for us to limit our sledding.

Not all our play was active and boisterous. Snails, as big as a cuffed adult fist, in pearly white shells roamed freely at the edge of the yard. We would each pick one at random, give it a name and root them on to see which would get first to a goal we set. The snails were not very cooperative and refused to move in a straight line. They would veer away in whatever direction they chose leaving a thick trail of slime behind. At other times we would try to coax the tortoise that lived around Errol's and Owah Moshe's house to come out of its shell and crawl about. We named him Sam-Sam. Sam-Sam proved to be very resistant to coaxing.

Chapter 15
Cassava Bread Baking Day

Tucko and Errol's mom made cassava bread about once every month. This was one of my favorite days to visit. I wished this happened more often for the action lasted all day. Mama, as we grew to call her, and a few other women would go to their farm to gather the cassava roots. I never saw the farms since they were located some distance away from the center of the village, but they must have been well tended for the women would return bent under the weight of their bulging quakes of cassava root. The quakes, made of reeds, were fashioned with a strap that was worn across the head with the basket portion resting on the back of the carrier.

The next steps were to scrape or peel and wash the roots, grate them, squeeze out the juice, pound the squeezed pulp into smaller bits, sift, and then bake the pulp into flat rounds on a giant iron griddle.

The most fun for us was to sit on the matapee pole to help drain the juice from the cassava pulp. A matapee is a long tube-like sieve made of woven reeds that is about six inches in diameter and four feet long. One end is open for filling; both the open and the closed ends have loops. After filling the matapee with the grated pulp the open end is hung from a beam on the ceiling, and a long sturdy pole is inserted into the loop at the closed end. The matapee is then slapped firmly throughout its length to get the cassava juice flowing. To obtain a completely dry pulp, one or two adults, sometimes helped by children, sit at one side of the pole to apply the pressure needed to squeeze the juice out into a container below. That was where we children did our best work.

It is of vital importance to drain the cassava pulp thoroughly since cassava bread is made with bitter cassava that contains significant amounts of cyanide (hydrocyanic acid, Encyclopedia Britannica) that could prove dangerous if ingested. Paralysis, and even death could occur. The cyanide is concentrated in the juice of the root. Bitter cassava has more of the toxic compound compared to sweet cassava which is safe to eat without further processing if boiled or cooked thoroughly.

Once the grated cassava is squeezed it is pounded into a course flour using a mortar, called a "mata" and pestle. The mortar at Errol's house was carved out of a tree trunk and the hollow was polished smooth from years of use. The pestle was at least four-foot tall and tapered from the bulb. The pounded flour is then sifted into a trough, also carved from a tree trunk. This coarse flour is then ready to bake. All the tools needed to produce this staple are basic kitchen supplies in Amerindian homes.

Mama, like most of the women in the village, baked her cassava bread into flat, crisp rounds on a large griddle. This was set on a circle of low rocks with a fire burning underneath. When the griddle was ready, Mama would place a generous scoop of the pounded pulp into the middle of the griddle then spread it evenly using a sturdy fan made of reeds until that side was baked. Then, with a skill born of years of practice, she would flip the bread over with her fan and bare hand to bake on the other side. Once done, whatever bread was not used that day would be laid out on the thatched roof of the hut to dry out and so preserve it longer. The bread would be shared among those who helped prepare it.

But cassava bread was not the only item made on bread-making day. Except for the skin, most of the by products from making cassava bread are used in some capacity. The juice from the cassava separates into a liquid layer and a starchy residue. The solid portion is used to make laundry starch, and the liquid is boiled down slowly for hours to make cassareep, a versatile seasoning sauce which is used in the preparation of meat and fish dishes, particularly a type of stew called pepper-pot. Pepper-pot is the national dish of Guyana and it is usually served with cassava bread. Even the scum that is spooned off during boiling of the cassareep is used to make a type of gravy.

Chapter 16
Chew and Spit

On one of our visits to Errol and Tucko's we saw a group of women and children gathered before a large pot. They passed around a calabash bowl of something that was dark brown and each of them would scoop up some of the brown stuff with the calabash spoon, chew it a little and then spit it into the pot. Errol's mother would swap the empty calabash bowl with a full one as needed. We watched a while and soon were invited to join in the process. The group shifted and made room for us.

As it turned out, we happened to visit on chew and spit day. At least that is what we called it. I am not sure if the Amerindians have a special name for the process, but chew-and-spit was the preliminary preparation for making bambali, or piwari, the local liquor.

Bambali is made from fermented cassava bread. The process involves soaking blackened pieces of the bread in sugared water, then chewing and spitting the mush out into a pot. When Errol's mom made cassava bread, I thought she accidentally burnt a few but she just baked them darker for making bambali. The chewed mush is emptied into a jug, and when full, the jug is covered and allowed to sit and ferment for days to produce the potent pinkish liquor. As I later learned, the enzymes in saliva help in the fermentation process. I do not believe anyone in the village knew the science behind the process, they just knew what was handed down to them for generations and that it worked.

This activity was a group effort and a time for socializing before the real party. Neighbors and relatives, mostly women and children, would come over to help chew and spit enough cassava bread to fill several jugs. I swallowed more of the sweet mush than I should have, but after our first try Roy and I became regulars on chew and spit day.

When the bambali was ready the group would again come, this time to celebrate, with men folk in attendance. Everyone would share a cup or two, passing it around the group for all to partake of the bambali. We were not permitted to attend the celebration parties, and with good reason, for even children were allowed sips of the liquor.

Music and dancing were rare during these celebrations. I only know of one Amerindian song, "Beeke dumma say..." that was sung during special celebrations, but not usually at times like this. Occasionally someone would play on the maracas or *shak-shak* as we called them, but mostly they drank and chatted for the bambali made folks more talkative than usual. It was one of the rare occasions where anyone spoke more than a few words.

I did not often hear traditional Amerindian singing, but some of my classmates had small transistor radios. It was from them that I first learned about western music, of bands such as The Beatles, and country singer Jim Reeves. We rarely listened to the music from England or America at home because the parents, especially Sister Enid, did not want us to be corrupted with ideas of young love and other such inappropriate thoughts. Although the Indian songs were mostly about love we did not understand a word of Hindi so that was all right.

It was the same when we saw the occasional movie when we visited the coast. Only Indian movies were allowed because at that time they had no kissing and other such lewd acts, according to the elders. There were plenty of suggestive actions and words, but I imagine those were believed to be veiled enough for us not to understand. The rules were the same even when I was a teenager, and the only English-speaking films I saw in Guyana were those shown when we had approved school shows, or Dracula movies, mostly with Christopher Lee. Lusting for blood was tolerated, lusting for flesh was not.

We saw a movie once in Orealla. The district commissioner had a screen and a projector, and he set these up in the school on a Saturday evening. I am not sure of how the projector was powered, perhaps it was battery operated, but we saw an English-speaking movie. The entire village turned out for the showing. I do not remember the title or contents of the film, but I do remember the excitement of that evening.

Chapter 17
Powis

During the school breaks, we would go on massive shopping sprees in the towns on the coast, mainly New Amsterdam which had big stores like J.P. Santos and Fogarty's that sold items in bulk, to stock up on non-perishables. We needed to purchase at least a four-month supply of rice, flour, sugar, salt, cooking oil, canned goods, spices, and other food staples each time. Kerosene oil, for the refrigerator, stove, and lamps, and batteries for the radio and flashlights also had to be stocked. Most of these items were not readily available, if at all, in Orealla for the Amerindians had a vastly different diet and household needs from us.

Toilet paper was also bought in bulk, but that was mostly for when the priest and his wife came to the mission. We only used the real thing when we ran out of newspaper. In fact, the volume of toilet paper relative to food products that we got on one trip prompted a clerk at J.P. Santos to remark that we apparently s—t more than we ate.

Most of our perishable food was sent to us by boat from Skeldon. Brother Maywah and Sister Marge helped with buying, preparing, and transporting the boxes of pre-cooked meat, fish and shrimp, and fresh vegetables to the boat. The usual vessel was Success but when she was not available Sea Queen made the delivery. These were the two main boats that traveled regularly from the coast near Skeldon to Orealla and Siparuta. Each had a roughly two-week schedule which could change without warning, and often did, so we needed to improvise if our supplies ran out before the next boat came. Sea Queen was primarily a sand boat that transported the abundant sand in Orealla and Siparuta for use on the coast. Sea Queen had room for a few passengers, but Success, captained by Mr. Sharma, was the main transport for the mail, passengers and supplies to the village.

Although we lived by a river which provided the village with fish it was not easy to obtain fish on demand. There was no marketplace where you could go to buy anything. Families fished for their own use and when they had a good catch, they would smoke and preserve the extra for later. On a few occasions we were able to obtain fish from a villager, but it was not something you could count on for there was no telling when anyone would go fishing. A fishing trip only happened when a family's supply was running low. Our family did not have the skills or time needed to secure enough of a catch for meals. More often the villagers would canoe off to the deeper waters and set a net or use several lines with hooks and fish all day, but the most interesting fish-catching method I observed was by spearing the fish. This often happened in the shallow waters near the shore. The fisherman, usually it was Errol's dad whom we observed, would stand completely still with the tip of his spear pointed down. Suddenly he would stab at the water and bring up the spear with a fish wriggling at the end. Not many fish were caught this way, it served only for a meal or two.

Once, when our shipped-in supply of fish and meat had run low and the boat was off schedule, Sister Enid decided to try cooking powis. This was a bird that we were not familiar with, but the Amerindians ate it. There were no farm animals other than a few chickens that families raised mostly for the eggs. The chief source of meat was wild game, labba, a large rodent, and bush hog being the most popular.

Sister Enid had asked to buy a chicken from a family who had a small flock, but they did not want to part with any. Later that day the father showed up with a bird. It was covered in black feathers and dead. He had shot it with an arrow. My sister reluctantly bought the powis after consulting with Delia. The two prepared the bird and started a powis curry that smelled heavenly.

Dinner time came and went, and the bird was still too tough to eat. My sister had heard that putting a clean, new nail into the pot could tenderize tough meat, so she did that. Soon she added another nail and then another. That made no difference still. That bird defied even the polished rock that was meant to soften it. Finally, tender or not, we had it for dinner. It was gamey and so tough that we could not chew it enough to swallow so we spat it out. That was the first and last time we had powis.

Chapter 18
Hog Ah Swim

One day, we saw the men of the village gather into canoes and row off down the river, all in the same direction. No one said a word. The men, armed with spears and axes, seemed to be in a hurry to get to the waterside, but no one ran, their gait was more like a purposeful power walk. And they did not take their individual canoes. There were at least two men to a vessel, and they rowed at a frantic pace. Soon there was a fleet of the small boats headed towards a singular unknown destination.

One of the first things I had noticed about the Amerindians is that they used very few words. Head movements could convey many messages with no need to speak. Depending on the angle of the chin, the direction and speed of the movement, and the nature of the eye contact one could extend a greeting, indicate approval or disapproval, give directions, communicate a lack of understanding, and give instructions to "follow me" among other messages.

Delia was not there to explain what was happening, and since it looked like something important was going on, Sister Enid asked a passer-by what the hubbub was about. Her answer was "hog ah swim". She seemed to believe that that should explain it all. We remained puzzled for hours until the canoes returned laden with blood-stained men and the carcasses of wild hogs.

As we later learned, wild hogs would occasionally gather and swim from one shore of the Corentyne river to the next, either from Guyana to Suriname or vice versa. This provided a rare opportunity for villagers to procure a sizeable quantity of meat without investing hours in hunting. Once the hogs were spotted, "word" would be spread to alert the men into action. They would row out and surround the hogs to trap them. Axes and spears were used to fell the game, and manpower to pull the haul into the canoes. The meat would be shared among the villagers who smoked and preserved what they did not use immediately. We were gifted a few hunks of meat by our neighbors. It was more of a success than powis.

I knew the Amerindians excelled in silent communication, but I was still surprised at the vocal reserve they displayed even through the palpable excitement generated when they knew the hogs were crossing the river and what would follow.

Chapter 19
Eddo

We also supplemented our food rations with local produce which was mainly root vegetables. Cassava, the sweet variety, not the cyanide-heavy bitter cassava, sweet potato, eddo, and yam, accompanied by plantain and dumplings were boiled then fried with seasonings to make a dish called simply, dry food. Salted codfish cooked with onions and tomatoes in butter was poured over this for a delicious meal. Delicious, that is, except for the eddoes.

I do not mind curried eddoes. Though a bit slimy, curried eddo tastes a little like an odd variety of Irish potato and the strong flavor and sauce masks the taste and dryness of the root. It was the boiled and fried version that I had difficulty swallowing. I found both the taste and the texture to be unappealing. Eddo tastes earthy and unless doused in butter sauce or some sort of gravy, it is dry. It would take me several cups of tea to swallow my portion down and even then, I would end up sitting with a few pieces of eddo on my plate desperately looking for a way to toss them. Sometimes stashing them in the cup worked but this was risky. We did not waste food in our house.

And that was why I dreaded seeing Mr. Chu come to our house with the tall Edger Boy biscuit tins. This had nothing to do with Mr. Chu himself; he was a perfectly nice gentleman. It was all about what was in the tins that troubled me.

Mr. Chu farmed in an area outside of the village and he was our main supplier of ground provisions, or root vegetables. Every so often he would bring us an assortment of produce and Sister Enid would eagerly buy whatever he came with. I always hoped to see a pineapple or two. If Mr. Chu had just one tin that was all good with me, but if he had two that was not – it meant more eddoes. Once, to my horror, one of the tins had nothing but eddoes. Memories of boiled eddo and mashed eddo and eddo in soup and curried eddo and eddo in stew, in place of Irish potato (what sacrilege) troubled me for a long time.

Chapter 20
The Ship comes in

After a steady diet of ground provisions, no sight was more welcome than Success. The coming of the boat meant that our longing for familiar foods would be satisfied, but it was an occasion of excitement for the entire village. It provided a break in the otherwise unchanging routine of each day. Those who lived up on chalk hill would be the first to spot the boat in the distance. Then, as if by some form of telepathy, there would be a silent trail of people, from both up and down-the-hill, heading towards the stelling. This was an event that both adults and children gathered to witness even if the boat came late at night.

There were usually several boxes for us and for Mr. Julius, the storekeeper. Since there was no reliable method to keep anything frozen on the boat, the food we received from the coast was usually precooked by Sister Marge. There would be parcels of fried fish, shrimp, steamed meat and poultry, a collection of newspapers that my brother would save for us, maybe a few magazines, and fresh vegetables. Vegetables that we were accustomed to were not available in Orealla. Among these were eggplant, okra, pumpkin, squash, Irish potatoes, and bora, a type of long string bean. The more perishable vegetables like spinach were precooked before shipping. Other than root provisions, vegetables were not a significant part of the Amerindian diet and were not cultivated. Cassava bread, fish, bush meat and the occasional iguana or turtle, and fruit comprised most of their diet.

If it had been a while since we had familiar foods Sister Enid would begin cooking right after receiving the boxes from the boat, even if it was night. Although we loved the canned meat that we sometimes had from the stocks we kept, which included delicacies such as Spam, Vienna sausages, corned mutton, Danish hot dogs, and sardines, we tried to conserve canned goods as much as possible for use when we had no other reasonable option. I still savor Vienna sausages cooked with onions and tomatoes.

Our only refrigerator was a medium-sized kerosene Electrolux, so the quantity of foods we could keep cold and unspoiled was limited. Brother Edward took special care to maintain the fridge in tip-top shape. He would clean the parts and trim the wick every weekend. He did the same with the lamps and he was the only one who handled the Tilley lamp with the delicate mantle that broke easily. When not in use the lamps sat on a high shelf in the living room with matches and a jar of purple methylated spirits at the ready. The spirits were used to preheat the Tilley lamp which we called "the gas lamp". It gave a brighter light than the hand lamps.

Success also brought the mail and even though mail call did not happen until the boat was unloaded no one left before then. Very few of the villagers received mail; most of their relatives and friends lived in Orealla or across the river on the Suriname bank of the Corentyne which was a short canoe ride away. Those who had children on the coast, whether in high school or working as domestic help, were the most eager for mail call but everyone shared in the excitement. Brother Edward usually did the honors, and he performed with a flourish. He would raise the envelope up high, squint as if he could not see the name, angle the letter a few times and then read out the addressee. I think the villagers enjoyed the build-up of excitement as they waited for the name to be read. At night, the process took two sets of hands, one to hold the flashlight or handlamp, and another to read the names.

Over the next few days, we would enjoy the special contents of the boxes. Brother Edward would read his newspapers, Sister Enid her magazines, and we children would enjoy any surprises included such as hard candies or a pack of cards.

Chapter 21
Nancy Story

Sister Enid worked hard. Besides teaching full time, she also cared for six children, cooked, baked and cleaned with limited conveniences. She usually had help from a girl who lived in the village, Delia is the one I most remember, but even so, it was a lot of work for two women to do. Clothes had to be washed using a hand-held beater with water obtained from rain barrels, or the river during a dry spell, and meals had to be cooked on a temperamental fireside whose efficiency depended on the quality and dryness of the wood available. The kerosene stove was used for cooking meals only when there was a lack of wood or when many dishes had to be prepared at once, such as when the priest visited, to conserve fuel. The oven was separate from the stove and was placed on the lit burners when baking. Skill and familiarity were required to control and monitor the temperature, and Sister Enid was an expert at this for she produced perfect cakes and pastries using this oven.

    During the week, after helping to bathe children, taking care of dinner and clean-up, Sister Enid often wrote her lesson plans while we did schoolwork or read. On weekend evenings she would darn clothes, knit intricate doilies, or become absorbed in any book she might have, such as Mills and Boon romances or Woman's Day magazines gifted to her by the priest's wife. On the occasions when she had none of that to do, she would have us gather around the hammock in the gallery where she lay with Joshua, who was a baby, and tell us Nancy stories. Squatting around the hammock and absorbing these stories are some of the most treasured childhood memories I have.

Nancy story is short for Anansi stories. Brer Anansi was a hero in African folklore who was introduced to Guyana by slaves. Soon these stories became part of the national culture and all stories told for entertainment became known as Nancy stories regardless of their content or origin. Some tales of Brer Anansi were included in those of our reading texts that were published in the Caribbean. Often there would be a lesson in these tales, similar to the morals in Aesop's fables.

A few of Sister Enid's stories were about Brer Anansi but the majority were of Hindu origin. Most were from the pages of the Hindu religious texts. Since my Aja's married sons and their families lived under his roof, my older siblings and cousins were present at the ceremonies he held in our backyard in Skeldon and often participated in them. Even when Aja, went to other homes to perform religious rituals, my siblings and cousins would accompany him. As a result, they were well versed in Hindu teachings and stories from the sacred texts.

As Sister Enid would say, when we sat listening to her stories you could hear a pin drop. The gallery had no lighting of its own and was bathed in the glow and shadows cast by the Tilley lamp on the dining room table which sat at an angle to the gallery. The gas lamp made a soft hissing sound as it burned. Because it shed a brighter light than the other oil lamps it would mainly be used for tasks that required stronger lighting, such as reading, darning clothes, or grading papers. Brother Edward, besides being headmaster also taught classes, so he did double duty and had paperwork from both positions to complete. He was usually absorbed in paperwork and was guaranteed peace and quiet from six young children during story time. The silence, except for the hiss of the lamp and an occasional night bird, the low lighting, whether from the moon or the lamp, and the dancing shadows cast by the bamboo leaves in the breeze, provided the perfect atmosphere for the fantastical tales that commanded our rapt attention.

Sometimes Sister Enid would drift off during the telling of a tale. We knew she was off track when she made random comments such as, "bring the broom from under the bed", or "when the fudge is cold use the sharp knife to cut it", that had nothing to do with the Maharani or Kumbhkaran, or ten-headed Ravana, or anything else in the story. A gentle shake accompanied by "mummy, you're sleeping", and a reminder of where she left off would get her back on track.

Another person who would tell us nancy stories was Uncle, Mr. Sharma's brother. Uncle would stay with us if he had business to take care of in Orealla. We knew him only by "Uncle". Uncle's business was usually related to procuring produce for sale, or for making arrangements to have logs shipped to Crabwood Creek.

Like Sister Enid, Uncle would sit in the hammock with an eager audience around him. His tales were more action oriented than my sister's, and his heroes were usually superheroes with names like Barstickalick and Steel Rail. His delivery was also more animated. Uncle would cuff the air and shout "bam, bam" or "pow, pow" when the characters were fighting, or clap his hands together and exclaim" baddam!" when the beaten bad man hit the ground.

Uncle could also whistle and would find a way to punctuate his stories with whistling. He would whistle a cheery melody when the hero was walking jauntily down the road minding his own business before being challenged by the bad man. Or whistles were used as secret codes by the hero and his friends. Uncle would tell us the secret codes before the characters used them so when he gave a long whistle followed by a short one, or three short whistles in quick succession we had to remember what they meant.

When Uncle would be winding down, we would always ask for one more story, then one more, and often would have to be chided to leave Uncle alone.

In later years, my eldest nephew Paschal, drew inspiration from some of the nancy stories Sister Enid told us, to start a series of Brer Anansi books. He created the stories but the tales we heard as children provided a starting point in his journey as an author.

Chapter 22
Chigger

No one wore shoes to school. No one that is, except for Caleb (not his real name) and the teachers. Caleb always wore yachtings, or canvas shoes. It was said that he had lost a few toes to a hungry piranha and that was the reason for his shoes. I never saw Caleb barefoot so I cannot attest to that, but it was the most likely explanation.

We were expected to wear socks and shoes at first. The boys had yachtings and I had a pair of black rubber Mary Janes. These set us apart from our classmates and made us uncomfortable. My nephews and I would head off for school before Sister Enid did and would leave the house with our socks and shoes neatly buckled and tied. This lasted as soon as we were out of her sight. The boys and I would remove the footwear, toss them under the house and scamper away. Only Dicky and Joshua could not do this, at least not at first. Since Dicky was younger, he left for school with his father and stayed in his father's class all day even though Brother Edward taught Fourth Standard. Sister Enid did notice our lack of shoes at school, and she tried to enforce wearing them but soon gave up. We were determined to fit in with the crowd.

Although the freedom of going shoeless allowed us to be better at running and climbing trees, it came with a few drawbacks. We were more prone to getting stuck with splinters and stubbing our toes on rocks and protruding tree roots, but worse of all, our feet became more vulnerable to chiggers.

Chiggers, known in the village as jigga, are the larval form of an arachnid called a trombiculid mite that latch on to the skin and burrow tiny holes with their jaw-like claws. They are found in every country. Once attached the larvae inject saliva to liquefy skin cells. They could remain on the skin for several days while they feed on the liquefied cells*3. Intense itching is the first symptom but then infection could occur. Infection was a given once we got a chigger bite.

We would try to hide the fact that we were bitten for as long as we could because the treatment was more dreadful than the bite itself. Our methods of washing and cleansing the bite by ourselves were not enough to prevent infection and soon the pain of the infected bite would cause us to limp. And then Sister Enid would know.

The treatment began with several of us gathering around the afflicted child. We knew our hands and even legs would be needed soon enough to hold down the flailing legs and arms, and buckling torso of the patient.

First, the infected boil would be broken with a safety pin or needle and the contents squeezed out. If the first attempt was not effective the boil would be lanced again. More than one attempt was a given since there were many misses as the patient tried to twist and kick throughout the procedure. If the removal was clean, a perfectly round white ball would be removed. If left to sit the ball would start to gently roll under the power of the living organism in it. Once the bite-hole was drained and cleaned with peroxide or methylated spirits, homemade M and B ointment that contained antibiotics, and soft grease would be applied. Soft grease is a type of soft wax that is shaped like a skinny candle and as far as I know, created for the very purpose of treating wounds. It was used mainly to prevent lockjaw. The treatment involved lighting the wick and having the hot grease drop directly into the wound to form an airtight seal. Clean bandages made of flour sacks were used to cover the area while the wound healed. As compensation for the ordeal the patient would be given an ice block made of heavily sweetened Kool-Aid that was frozen in ice cube trays.

Sister Enid always stressed to us the importance of taking good care of wounds to prevent the onset of the dreaded lockjaw. And she stressed it every time we were treated for a wound. As she told us, when she was a child in Skeldon she knew a man who had lock jaw. He had stepped on a rusty nail, and the puncture wound was not treated properly. The wound was not drained, and no soft grease was applied. Now this man, his face and neck became all twisted, the rest of his body jerked with spasms, and he could not even scream because his jaw was clamped shut. Forever. Then he died. Sometimes Sister Enid would try to demonstrate how his face and neck and body writhed to make sure we grasped the seriousness of lockjaw.

Sister Enid was also particular about how a sewing needle should be put away. It must be threaded with a long piece of thread with a large knot tied at the end, immediately after use. Needles were not to be left anywhere but in the sewing box. As she told us, when she was a child in Skeldon she knew a woman who stepped on a needle that had no knotted thread. The needle entered her vein and travelled throughout her body, poking her as it went along, causing the woman to scream for dear life at every poke. Finally, the needle reached her heart and became stuck there. Then she died. This story scared me even though it seemed a bit far-fetched, but decades later I read of Henry Frick, a New York industrialist, whose toddler daughter swallowed a pin and suffered untold pain until she died at age five. This was just a few years before X-rays came into common use.

Sister Enid's story had enough of an impact that, to this day, I always thread a needle with a large knot at the end immediately after use, then put it in the sewing box right away.

Over the next few days after the initial treatment, the chigger bite would be washed, cleaned with methylated spirits and M and B ointment would be applied. Sister Enid, like many mothers, made her own antibacterial ointment. The local pharmacist, Mr. Bovill in Skeldon, would give the recipe if one did not already know it. The M and B in the ointment were two antibiotics, I believe they were mycitracin and bacitracin, and they came in pill form. Sister Enid would pound the chalk-like pills in the recommended ratio using a small mortar and pestle and mix the resulting powder with Vaseline. This mixture was applied to all bites or sores that we had, and we suffered from many. The populations of insects in the village, like mosquitoes or sand flies and others that we had no name for, thrived in an area with no deterrents like insecticides and we were ready targets. The Amerindians did not seem to be as affected as we were, and I can only guess that they must have developed some resistance over generations of facing these species.

Besides the M&B ointment, soft grease, and methylated spirits Sister Enid had other remedies that helped us survive our childhood.

Vicks Vapor Rub was the go-to for chest colds and flu. Besides rubbing it on our chests and noses, according to the directions on the label, Sister Enid would also have us swallow a chunk of it. This last bit was not on the label but nearly every mother I know in Guyana used this method to treat a chest cold. Regardless of what the manufacturer suggested, we healed quickly and not one of us has yet died from swallowing the product. I am not recommending that anyone try this, I am just stating what we did.

For coughs, there was the dreaded Buckley's Cough Syrup, a thick white concoction that looked like runny school glue. The acrid taste lingered on your tongue, and the burn lingered in your esophagus long after you managed to swallow a tablespoon down. This product also did not fail us, it worked.

God bless the person who encased drops of Seven Seas Cod Liver Oil in a form that you could swallow and not suffer drinking the oil and have it coat your mouth and have the taste linger for hours. There are some people who exist that do love slurping the oil. I have a cousin in this category. She is a perfectly fine human being, but I cannot understand her preference for sipping cod liver oil.

The medicines we hated the most were the ones many a Guyanese mother would refer to as "cleaning out." Decades later, a conscientious grandmother mentioned to an American physician that she believed her grandsons needed some cleaning out. The physician made clear his views when he asked, "Cleaning out? Why? Are they pipes?" One could argue that the intestines do have a pipe-like structure, but it did not seem wise to bring that up with a trained physician who had many certificates on his wall, some with Latin words and everything.

Unlike most medicines we took, the effects of the cleaning out variety did not last for a few minutes, they lasted all day and restricted our wanderings to within running distance of the outhouse. Senna pod tea and Epsom salts were the most common ones. I preferred to take Epsom salts. This involved downing about an ounce of the strong salt mixture. I would hold the medicine in one hand and a glass of extra sweet sugar water in the other. A quick gulp of the salts followed by the sugar water made the agony last for under a minute. Senna tea, on the other hand, felt like I was being slowly poisoned. A cup of strong brewed senna pods was sweetened with milk and sugar and placed before you. It looked like our typical Red Rose tea, but the smell, taste and effects were far from the delicious comfort of Red Rose. I would vomit often and could not face regular tea for at least a week afterwards. One had to be careful with the vomiting for if Sister Enid saw she would add more to your cup to make sure you got the full dose.

The greatest puzzle to me, however, was why, when there was only one outhouse, did we all receive "cleaning out" on the same day.

Chapter 23
Breaking Bread

Tabu, a fish stew, and cali, the local name for cassava bread, were eaten every day by the Amerindians, but occasionally there would be treats such as labba, other bush meats, iguana, or turtle.

One day, while a few of us were playing under the almond tree by the river, we spotted a three-foot iguana, or guana as it was called, in the bamboo patch nearby. Errol told us to stop playing and to be quiet as he ran to tell his father. Soon they both came back. The guana had moved but was still visible among the leaves. We all watched in open-mouthed silence as Errol's father took aim, pulled back his bow and shot the iguana with the first arrow. It would be the only shot he would have been allowed. If he had missed, the guana would have made its escape. The animal fell to the riverbank below and Errol retrieved it with the arrow still stuck through its middle.

A day or so later I was playing with Tucko when her grandfather, Owah Moshe, invited us to come up to eat. He gave us two bowls of what looked like stew, and cali. I was hesitant because of Sister Enid's stern warnings not to eat foods we did not know about because we could get kinna. I knew that kinna meant that one would break out with something terrible like painful sores all over. However, after seeing Tucko dig in I did the same. It turned out to be iguana stew.

There was another occasion where I braved eating a dish that I was hesitant to try. It was turtle soup. I assumed it was a water turtle that either Owah Moshe or his son had caught so I joined Errol and Tucko as they ate. I never did find out if it was a water turtle, but I never saw Sam-Sam again.

None of these dishes was memorable. I cannot recall what they tasted like and that was probably because I was consumed with worry, about whether I would get kinna, as I ate. In later years I realized that the word referred to an allergic reaction that manifests on the skin.

Sister Enid told us all about kinna. As a child in Skeldon, she knew of a woman who got kinna from eating something that was strange to her. Her whole face swelled up like a bladder (bladder was our word for balloon) and white spots broke out all over her body; her face, arms, legs and everywhere else was covered. She was a woman of darker complexion and people could see her polka dotted body coming down the road from a mile away. The swelling went down, but that woman had to live with that skin until the day she died. So, if we did not want polka dotted skin 'til Thy kingdom come we were to avoid unfamiliar foods, especially from strangers.

Before Delia, Anna used to help us with the housework until she married and had her own family to take care of. We children so wanted to try tabu, made with fish, and cali that Anna, after checking with Sister Enid, brought us some from home. We loved it, and none of us developed the dreaded kinna, so Anna would treat us to this dish from time to time. Anna's tabu and cali had won my sister's seal of approval.

Chapter 24
Flying High

Easter was kite flying time. From about a month before, the children of the village would be consumed by activities related to making and flying kites.

During drawing time at school all our artwork would feature kites. We did not have formal art classes. Only core subjects like English, Mathematics, History, Geography, and Science were taught but we were given drawing time which meant we should take out our unlined exercise books and draw something. Pupils who did not have unlined books would "borrow" sheets from those who did. The girls tended to focus on making their kites pretty with frills and tongues and intricate roses in the middle. The boys would forgo frills and roses, but tongues were important for they made a flapping noise in the wind, the bigger the better for then the flapping would be louder and more intimidating. They often drew razor blades at the end of the tails to indicate how fierce their kites would be. Reality mimicked art for when we made our kites, we based them on the pictures we had drawn.

Mr. Julius tailored his stocks to cater to this annual passion. His shop brought in tissue paper in every color imaginable. Everyone called it kite paper for that was all we ever used tissue paper for. He also stocked up on thick thread and kite string. He need not have worried about glue because we used pasee, a berry that oozed a sticky paste when squeezed. It grew wild, was effective, and free. Brother Edward must have been especially thankful for pasee berries for it meant that we would not be tempted to get into his glue.

That glue was a precious commodity for Brother Edward made it himself from gum arabic. He would soak chunks of the hardened amber sap in water until it dissolved, sometimes this took several days, then strain it through a fine cloth to remove the impurities. Stirring in a tablespoon of glycerin completed the process. The jar of glue had a red rubber bung stopper and that, along with a brush used only for the glue, sat on a high bookshelf, and was only taken down for important tasks such as to bind books or secure packages. If pasee berries were scarce we would make a paste of flour and water but that was not as desirable for it was not light and transparent like pasee glue.

Mothers were also prepared. They saved their old coconut brooms so that we could use the tough but light broom sticks to frame our kites. Brooms were made from coconut leaves. The soft green parts of the leaves were stripped from the spine in the middle. When enough of the spines were collected, a comfortable handful for an adult, they would be tied at the thicker end with a strong strip of cloth or string. The soft, new brooms were used indoors at first but as they wore down to the tougher middle portion of the spines, they would become yard brooms. The stiffer and stronger yard brooms, near the end of their usefulness except for being burnt for fuel, were given to us for our kites. Mothers would also save old clothing for us to use as kite tails.

It took skill and great patience to create a perfectly symmetrical kite frame. The central point of the kite where all the broomsticks crossed had to be firmly secured in the proper orientation with a thin string or tibisiri straw, then the perimeter would be bordered with heavy cotton thread. The broomsticks had a tendency to wobble as you tried to tie the border and the best solution was to put a knee at the hub as you worked. Fresh pasee berries would then be squeezed over the thread and broomsticks before the tissue paper was applied. Most of us opted to put a different color of tissue paper in each of the six sections even though it took longer to finish our kite. Tongues, frills, roses and other decorations, and a cloth tail would then be added. We were not allowed to use razor blades.

The favorite spot to fly our kites was the field behind the nurse's home and in front of Mr. Julius' shop. It was a wide, grassy expanse with no trees. Two of us needed to work together to get a kite properly off the ground; one of us would hold the kite aloft while the other ran with the string wound around a twig. The runner would unwind the string and shout "let go" when it was time to release the kite.

The skeletons of kites that met their demise in the treetops was a common sight for months after Easter.

Chapter 25
Christmas and Shove Down

We spent one Christmas vacation in Orealla. The Christmas break was one of those times when we would head for the coast for a few weeks over the holidays, but Sister Enid and Brother Edward wanted us to experience the holidays in Orealla at least once.

We brought a western spin, common on the coast, to the festivities. Those on the coast who set up a Christmas tree usually had an artificial one that was imported since it was not possible to obtain a live fir or spruce tree in tropical Guyana. The villagers were excited to assist with the preparations for Christmas celebration at the school. Sister Enid directed the process. Instead of an artificial tree, the villagers and a group of teachers scouted out the perfect tree to decorate for Christmas. They cut and transported it and set it up in the middle of the Prep A area of the school. It almost touched the ceiling.

We did not have regular classes on the day the teachers decorated the tree. None of us could concentrate on lessons when such exciting things were happening around us. A few of the fourth standard children and teachers supervised us as we watched the tree being transformed, and when it was drawing time, we all drew elaborate Christmas trees.

The female teachers did most of the decorating, but the males climbed the ladder to reach the higher branches. First, the decorators spread the stretched-out cotton bolls on the branches to mimic snow. We brought some of the cotton bolls from the coast, and some were donated by villagers who had cotton trees. I do not believe that many, or any, of the native children who stood watching the snow on the tree that day have ever seen the real thing.

Some local hand-made decorations, crafted from reeds and tibisiri were hung on the branches, but it was the delicate shiny balls in many shapes and colors, and the glittering tinsel and garlands, which were new to many, that made us stand in awe. A large cardboard cut-out Nativity Scene, brought from the coast, stood prominently beside the tree.

On the last day of school, we celebrated the holiday. We faced the tree and sang Christmas Carols that we had practiced for weeks with Mr. Penn. We belted out each tune with gusto, for though we might not have known about sleighs or snow or mistletoe, we were caught up in the merriment of the season and gave it our all.

Each child was given a paper bag of treats and trinkets. Hard candies, a piece of pound cake, colored pencils, and sharpeners were among the presents. No colorful wrapped gifts were laid under the tree. This was not a common practice in Guyana. Even when we left Orealla for the coast and set up a Christmas tree each year we never gift-wrapped presents and placed them under it. When we were very young, we received small gifts, usually guns and dolls which were handed directly to us, unwrapped, but later our present would be a trip or two to the movies.

On Christmas morning we went to church and later had a special holiday meal of chicken curry, rice, and cake. There were usually two kinds of cake, pound cake and fruit cake, both of which Sister Enid made from scratch. Christmas celebration was low-key for the Amerindians. If it were not for the party at school the holiday might have been the same as any other day except for those who went to church.

Although Christmas was not an occasion for major celebration in Orealla, heralding in the New Year was a different story. The festivities started on Old Year's Day. Much bambali would be consumed as the men traveled from house to house where they would be offered a drink or two, before the Shove Down started later that evening. This may have been the one time when I heard the villagers raise their voices in a shout. The parade of mostly men wound through the village pathway with shouts of "Shove Down". The shouts were accompanied by a pushing motion. They were shoving down the old year and making room to welcome in the new one with its promise of new possibilities and hope.

Chapter 26
Owah Moshe

Owah Moshe, Owah means grandfather in the Arawak language and Moshe is an endearing form of Moses, was Errol's and Tucko's grandfather on their father's side. He lived next door to his son, Errol's father, and his family. Errol's home was an open thatched hut with an earthen floor throughout the living areas. Only the sleeping quarters had a wooden floor, and this was raised a few inches off the ground. This area was walled off. The walls were made from slats of manicole palms with many creases between the slats. There were no inner walls and uncovered openings cut into the outer walls served as windows. The overhanging eaves of thatch protected against the elements. Most Amerindian homes had a similar layout.

In contrast, Owah Moshe's house stood on stilts. It had an outside stair-case, and wooden walls and floors. The house was fashioned much like ours, which belonged to the Anglican diocese, but his was smaller. Since Owah Moshe was a catechist of the church, it is possible that his home may have been subsidized by the Mission.

His yard had a few cotton trees from which Mama obtained some of the cotton that she used to make thread for weaving hammocks on her loom. There was also a tree favored by butterflies and we came every day to watch the caterpillars evolve through all the life stages and eventually become butterflies that flew away. The inside of Owah Moshe's house was sparsely furnished; it had a dining table and chairs, and a large Bible and a Book of Common Prayer sat on a shelf. Dining sets were not a common sight in Amerindian huts; benches and low stools were the usual furniture.

Owah Moshe's main duties as catechist included managing the church and conducting services when the priest was away. He also officiated at funerals and was one of the first persons, besides Captain, also called Toshao, to be informed of happenings in the village. Owah Moshe would ring the church bell to share news with the people. A cheerful peal indicated a happy occasion, such as the birth of a child, a slow "dooong, dooong" told of a death and a loud, rapid ringing indicated an emergency or some other unexpected occurrence. The only time I heard that rapid peal was when the murders on the river took place.

Besides handling church administration duties, Owah Moshe also served as one of the local medics. Although there was a resident trained nurse from the coast who was stationed in the village, the Amerindians were more comfortable using traditional treatments administered by local practitioners to cure their illnesses. Owah Moshe was familiar with making poultices and knew what natural brews to use for a variety of ailments. If there was a condition that he was not familiar with, only then he would refer the patient to the nurse. Modern medicine was a last resort.

There was a medical officer employed by the government who visited on occasion. Everyone called him Doc. His role was mostly administrative. He was usually dressed in what could best be described as safari clothes. His well-pressed khaki shirt would be tucked into his belted, well-pressed khaki shorts and he would wear a khaki-colored cork hat with a brown leather chin strap. Socks and shoes, or black Wellington boots if it rained, would complete his outfit. Doc would often consult with Owah Moshe and would leave Orealla laden with curative herbs such as lemon grass, sage, sweet broom, and leaf-of-life.

The priest presided over baptisms and weddings when he visited. Both were occasions that were accompanied by much festivity, but they were not very frequent. The Amerindians continued their traditional practice of marriage by the couple moving in together with the blessings of the parents and the Toshao, even if they did attend Sunday services. Sometimes, however, Owah Moshe would be able to persuade a couple to baptize a child or to get married in the church. I believe he would have been a better choice to conduct weddings rather than the English priest, for he would not have been as surprised when a ceremony had to be halted just before the vows were said so that the bride could nurse her wailing baby.

Chapter 27
Open Wide

Medical care in the village was covered by the nurse, the medical officer, and local practitioners like Owah Moshe. Dental care was limited to extraction, when the pain could no longer be tolerated, with a pair of pliers, or by a pulling on a string tied to the tooth. This was usually done by anyone who had the stamina to conduct the procedure.

A dentist, commissioned by the government, visited Orealla for a few days while we were there. Our family was familiar with Dr. Dean. He lived in Skeldon and had tended to our dental needs a few times. They were mostly extractions of broken teeth that Sister Enid could not get a grip on to pull out. We received a numbing agent, the administration of which was frightening enough considering the length of the needle, but nearly as upsetting was having to look at Dr. Dean's face as he did the extraction. The pressing of his lips and focused demeanor as he tried to get a grip on the small portion of tooth that was left was not a comforting sight. Then we watched him squeeze and yank with all his might. Why I never closed my eyes, like I do now when I visit the dentist, I would never know.

Sister Enid and Brother Edward warned us not to share our experiences at the dentist with our friends as soon as we learned of Dr. Dean's pending visit. It was difficult to stay silent knowing the fate that was in store for those unsuspecting souls, but we managed. We had to, or the consequences would have been dire. No one wanted the dentist to visit all the way from the coast and then have no one show up. But it was not easy to keep silent on the one topic we knew more about than our Amerindian friends. It was our only opportunity to share our superior knowledge and we were warned to stay silent.

The day arrived and everyone came to school accompanied by their parents. A few parents were recruited to help if needed. As if there was any question that extra hands would be required to keep heads and arms and feet still while the dentist practiced his sworn profession.

First up were the youngest children. Most had already lost several baby teeth and needed no procedure done. Everything went well until Dr. Dean tried to extract a molar from a particularly strong lad. He flailed at and slapped and kicked the dentist before he was restrained, head and arms, torso, and legs. His appearance after the procedure did not help reassure the rest of the students that everything was going to be alright. The young man's face was misshapen with one cheek swollen and padded full of cotton, and there were still bloodstains down his chin.

Then the crying started. Slowly a wave of quiet whimpering traveled down the line, then it became louder sobs and bodies shook with fear. Even the parents seemed unsure of continuing with the visit, but the persuasive powers of the nurse and the staff managed to convince them that it was a good thing. Parents and staff were able to halt a few attempted escapes, and the foiled escapees were the next to receive treatment.

Dr. Dean was supposed to have carried out exams and treatments over a couple of days, but he decided to examine everyone and finish the worst cases on the first day. He did not expect that anyone would show up again and no one did.

Chapter 28
Buck

Except for a few occasions we spent the longer school breaks, late June through August, and Christmas through New Year, with relatives on the coast.

In Skeldon we stayed at Brother Maywah and Sister Marge's home. Their four children were around our age, so we had a lot of playmates. All the children slept on ground beds, created by spreading blankets on the hardwood floors wherever there was room. The ten of us would whisper long into the night and play games, most of which we made up. During the day while the adults worked, we could roam the neighborhood so long as we promised to be careful and not wander off too far, or explore the backyard, which was laden with fruit trees, and try to catch butterflies and dragonflies, which we called chin. At one point the family owned a pet toucan that had half its beak missing. Someone had found it during a trip to the interior and gave it to my brother. The toucan lived on a perch in the backyard close to the house. The family cared for it as best they could, but it was difficult for the bird to survive with half a beak that became infected. We heard that it had later died.

We spent most of the vacation time in Port Mourant where Brother Edward's family lived. The sleeping arrangements, on a huge ground bed, were the same as at Brother Maywah's house, but the family situation was different. In years past two brothers had married two sisters, one couple was Brother Edward's parents. His family occupied the lower flat of the house while his aunt and uncle lived upstairs. Both brothers had died but the wives still occupied the house. The women were both grandmothers and called Ajee, the Hindi word for grandmother on one's father's side. To differentiate, we called them Upstairs Ajee and Downstairs Ajee.

Although my nephews' grandmother was Downstairs Ajee we slept upstairs because there was more room. Uncle Richard, Brother Edward's brother, continued to manage the bookshop started by his father. The shop took up half of the downstairs area of the house.

For us children these were fun-filled days, but I am not sure that it was the same for the adults. Upstairs Ajee had six grandchildren who lived in the house with their parents, so a dozen young children had to be cared for and monitored. We would together explore the marketplace, which was nearby, and when we visited the bookshop, R.H.Makhanlall Bookstore, and started fiddling with the books Uncle Richard would give us a penny each to get three-for-penny butterballs from the local shop. It was worth the cost to get us away from being underfoot.

We were sure to be in Port Mourant for the August horse races. August Monday was special; everyone had new clothes, and sometimes new shoes, Bata shoes if you were lucky, to attend the races. I suppose the actual racing was fun for those who knew the horses or betted on them, but for most it was mainly a social occasion, a time to dress up and show off your new outfit, and picnic, and flirt if you were old enough. I enjoyed the social atmosphere, but I found the racing to be tedious. If it rained racing would be delayed until the weather cleared, and then I would have to give up my front row position along the track to avoid the mud that the horses would splash. If it did not rain the August sun could be unforgiving. And even if the weather was perfect my interest would wane with each false start, which far exceeded the races that were run, in number and in length of time.

None of us knew then that we would one day be living in the housing compound that bordered the racecourse. The British administrators who lived in those homes returned to England after Guyana became independent in May of 1966, and the supervision of the sugar estates fell to the Guyanese government. We moved to Port Mourant later that year and settled into one of those houses.

It was during the time we spent on the coast that we were often called Buck, the derogatory name for Amerindians. It held connotations of being primitive, but especially of being stupid. If we would happen to do something silly, we were told that we were acting like Buck, or that we were "stuppid like Buck", and if we were quiet, we were dubbed "dumb head Buck.".

We were too young to verbalize the intelligence the Amerindians displayed in the context of their own culture. They did not have the freedom to attend secondary school like pupils on the coast did, so many lacked the learning that would have elevated them to the status of "smart" as defined by those outside of their world. Since secondary schools were located only on the coast, the Amerindians would have to find a place to stay, and pay for room and board in addition to school fees. These expenses were beyond the reach of most residents of Orealla so there was little drive to strive towards an education beyond forth standard.

During our time in Orealla there were two pupils whose performance in the Common Entrance exams earned them scholarships to secondary schools on the coast. Brother Edward saw their potential and took both under his wing and gave them extra lessons. Jillian, who sometimes spent the night with us when lessons ran late, was one who worked hard towards this goal, and Horatio, son of Mr. Chu was the other. Horatio passed the Common Entrance exam and won a scholarship to the most prestigious high school for boys in Guyana, Queen's College in Georgetown. Afterwards he attended university in the United Kingdom to study engineering. Unlike their fellow classmates, each of these students was able to afford a place to stay on the coast.

Wealthier families in the coastal towns sometimes employed Amerindian women as domestic workers. These women would live with the family and did whatever the mistress requested. Many families were kind, but there were often reports of abuse of these young women who were far from home with no social support they could count on. Delia had worked for a family on the coast before she returned to Orealla and then came to help us. It was not uncommon to hear the phrase, "they have a Buck girl", and that needed no further explanation.

Chapter 29
Tete Sofia

I tried hard to heed Sister Enid's warning to stay close to home. Very hard. I knew of the dangers that lurked everywhere, but there were times when I became so fascinated by the things around me that I lost track of how far I had wandered off.

There was no end of things to grab and hold one's attention. I would come upon a shame baby bush and touch each frond and watch it close and droop. The scientific name of what we called shame baby is *Mimosa pudica,* as I learned in later years, and this trait most likely developed and persisted to protect the plant from being eaten. The closed leaves would appear to be unappetizing to animals and they would leave the shrub alone. At times I would be distracted by the sight of a mora seed that had washed to shore. A mora seed is the size of an adult fist and has the shape and smooth, dark red coat of a kidney bean. Depending upon the site where I spotted the seed, it could mean a walk down a slippery slope to the river, the river that we were warned to avoid because it had piranha and water snakes.

Sometimes I would wander by a hut where women were baking cali, or weaving a hammock on a loom, or making baskets using dyed reeds, and I would stop to watch. No one seemed to consider this strange. If there were children whom I knew I would stay to play a spell, maybe a few games of jacks, using smooth stones or seeds. Or I would join them in enjoying cookrit or wara, which was our name for the fruit of the awara palm.

There was a place on Chalk Hill where there was a sheer drop to the river below. A white sandy beach was exposed when the tide was low, but at high tide there would be eddies at the bottom. If you looked at the swirling eddies long enough, you would become dizzy and risk falling off the cliff. For some reason we thought this was fun and the boys, their friends, and I did it often.

On one of these wanderings, I ended up at the very end of the village, the northern edge of Chalk Hill, where Tete Sofia lived. Tete means grandmother in the Arawak language, and Sofia might have been Sophia but was pronounced So-Fie-Ah. I had seen Tete Sofia many times down the hill. Sometimes she attended church, or would go to get something from Mr. Julius' shop, but mostly she just wandered around. She walked with a long stick, taller than she was, and kept her head bowed as if she was looking for something on the ground. Although we sidestepped her for her strangeness no one feared her.

I did not know that I had stumbled upon Tete Sofia's home. I just knew that she lived somewhere up chalk hill, but when she emerged from her hut, she was easily recognizable because of her walking stick and her gait. I was some distance away from the clearing in which her hut stood, partially hidden by shrubbery, and instinct told me to stay where I was. I did not fancy her seeing me, given her odd behavior.

If I thought Tete Sofia's behavior was strange when I saw her down the hill, that was nothing compared to what I was about to witness. There were two rain barrels made from steel drums standing close to her hut. One was covered and it most likely contained water, but the other was empty. Tete Sofia raised her face skyward, said something which I could not hear, then stuck her head in the empty steel drum and began to preach.

Not all of what she said was coherent, but she invoked the wrath of God upon Sidom. I had attended church long enough to think that Sidom was Sodom, as in Sodom and Gomorrah. Her voice was magnified by the drum and developed an eerie, sonorous, quality as she cursed the devil and all his works and told him to "get thee hence".

She punctuated her sermon by frequently banging on the empty drum with her walking stick. When her head was not in the drum Tete Sofia would walk around stabbing the ground with her stick as she stressed a point or felled an enemy of the Lord, or she would stop, look upwards and raise her shaking arms to the heavens, stick and all.

I am not sure how long I stood there but I was rooted to the spot, unable to take my eyes off the scene before me. Finally, I found myself running down the hill. I passed the black water creek from which I had intended to drink but did not stop running until I reached home.

I do not know if I was ever in danger, but it was possible. Tete Sofia might have been in a state where she was not in total possession of her senses. Perhaps she had used some herbs that had the effect of transporting her into an alternate reality, and maybe if she had seen me my appearance may have triggered some unwelcome impulses. Who knows what she might have conceived me to be?

I did not tell anyone of what I had seen for a long time. For once I wished that I had obeyed Sister Enid's warnings (not that I deliberately disobeyed, mind you). Ever since that day I did not dismiss Tete Sofia as a harmless, strange old woman. I feared her. I began to wonder whether her walking stick was to assist her in walking or if she saw it as a staff, like the ones people carried in the Bible.

There was another odd person I remember. At communion, he would cup his wafer in his hand and pretend to eat it but did not. Then after church he would go about the village raising the wafer for all to see and proclaim, "God's food. Body of Christ. Lamb of God." I started to avoid him also.

Chapter 30
Milk-and-Biscuit

Every day at school each child would receive a ladle of milk and two biscuits. This nutritional supplement was provided by UNICEF and distributed by the government to school children in areas of need.

The consumption of milk was minimal in the Amerindian diet. There were a few cows, but I only distinctly remember one because of the way in which it died.

Our milk supply at home consisted mainly of cans of Carnation Evaporated milk, and Borden Sweetened Condensed milk that came from contented cows, according to the label. I still love both today and although they taste the same, the enjoyment is diminished because they are no longer a treasured commodity that needs to be rationed. Powdered milk was substituted when our supplies of canned milk ran low.

At around two o' clock in the afternoon pupils would line up, the younger classes first, for milk and biscuits. No one said biscuits in the plural, it was always milk-and-biscuit spoken as one word. Each child had to bring a cup from home, usually an enameled cup, the type that is used for camping in the United States. Nearly every cup was dented and flaked, but as long as it did not leak, we did not care. Staff members, and some of the older students, would reconstitute the powdered milk in large white enamel buckets. Some would ladle the milk or hand out biscuits while others supervised the lines. I once heard a student ask for a biscuit to take home for a younger sibling. It must have been difficult for the teacher to deny the request.

When we were given the polio vaccine, we received Kool Aid and biscuits with cream, instead of milk-and-biscuit that day as a special treat. I do not know if there was some strategy to this since the visit of the dentist was still fresh in everyone's mind, and no one knew what the drops would taste like. Our experience with the taste of medicine was not pleasant. If it did not initiate gagging, like senna tea, it was bitter, like Epsom salts, or it set fire to your tongue like ginger tea. Only the green Antipar syrup tasted sweet.

The administration of the vaccine went much faster than the dentist's visit. There were three lines instead of one, and all we had to do was open our months and the nurse or her helpers would squirt sweet, pink drops onto our tongues. There were a few pupils who refused to open their mouths at first, but after seeing the smiles of those who had their drops it was easy to get them to cooperate. Then we went back to class for Kool Aid and cream biscuits which were waiting at our desks. It was drawing time when we were done, and we all drew pictures of smiling children lining up to receive their polio drops.

There was one child in the village who was paralyzed from polio. This happened before the mass vaccination effort. She used a leg brace and crutches to get around and received ready help from everyone when needed.

Chapter 31
Original Sinners

Snakes abounded. I had more encounters with them than I should have mainly because I would go wandering off without fear, lost in my thoughts as I concentrated on what was before me, and forget about all the warnings of the dangers around.

One day I was picking peppers from a low bush that stood behind Mr. James' house. Mr. James was a teacher from the coast who occupied the mission house next to ours. Even after he left Orealla that house was forever more called Mr. James' house, at least by us. No one told me to pick peppers; I just happened to pass by and saw that the tree was loaded with them. I tied the hem of my dress into a makeshift pocket and started picking. Suddenly a form darted at me and drew back. I had not heard a sound and were it not for its flicking pink tongue I may not have even seen the snake stretched along a branch. It was the same green shade as the pepper plant, and it lay still. God may have given the snake that color to blend in and avoid danger, but he gave me fear and adrenalin to help me escape danger. I backed away a few steps, dropped the peppers and ran. Delia told me that it was a parrot snake when I described it to her. Parrot snakes are poisonous.

Another memorable snake encounter happened at home. After they were finished cooking and the fireside had cooled, Delia and my sister would daub it with wet clay. Daubing the fireside made it look brand new; the clay sealed the cracks, smoothed the surface, and covered the soot stains. Several pots of wet clay were stored on a shelf below the house and one day I was asked to fetch one. I ran down and grabbed a pot, not noticing the brown coil around the bottom. My sudden action must have surprised the snake for it did not have time to be alerted and get into attack mode. It just fell off the pot and landed on the earthen floor. By the time the adults ran downstairs in response to my scream it was nowhere to be seen.

The possible near encounter with a snake that gives me the most chills however was the one that Roy spotted. If he was not home sick from school that day I might have had my closest contact with a snake yet. We had come home for lunch, as was the practice for the entire school, and Sister Enid looked in on Roy. He seemed fine so she comforted him then went about helping to get lunch together. At first, she ignored his "mummy, come" pleas, since she had just checked on him. When he said, "mummy come, something is moving", she told him he must have been dreaming and to try and go back to sleep. After his third cry she went into the room to give him the attention she thought he was seeking. He pointed to the ceiling and said something was moving there. The movement was right above my bed. When Sister Enid saw the snake, she grabbed Roy, shooed us all into the gallery, and sent for help.

Several men came, armed with long bamboo poles. We were admonished to stay in the gallery and not come close. When they were done, a brown and black snake, about eight feet long in my estimation, lay dead on the ground by the stairs. It was a labaria. The labaria is a member of the pit viper family and is highly venomous. It is one of the most feared snakes in Orealla.

There were many occasions when we would see snakes on our way to school, or while playing, in the grass or in trees. We were warned to check for snakes before entering the outhouse, no easy feat at night with just a flashlight so we avoided night visits if that was at all possible. Although I was scared at each encounter, I was not filled with the kind of dread I now feel at the sight of a snake. That came after Errol was bitten.

Chapter 32
Pests

None of us children managed to leave Orealla without at least one marabunta sting that caused our eye to be swollen shut. For days. And no one even batted an eye, pun intended, for it was so commonplace.

Marabunta wasps, or Jack Spaniards as some called them, are reddish brown with touches of black. They are about two inches long and build papery nests with many compartments, usually in sheltered spots. We would often not notice a nest until after the first sting, then it seemed as if the entire nest emptied and chased after you. It is said that if one stands still the wasps would be less prone to sting. Many have heard this theory, but I know of no one who has tested it, and I was not going to be the first. The sting is painful, and although they can attack any part of the body it seemed to me that most children were stung near the eye. I do not know of an instance where a marabunta sting caused anything more serious than pain and massive swelling. Ice was scarce with only three refrigerators in the village and so the treatment was usually just washing with water. Sister Enid would often apply a dab of alcohol. The Amerindians had been dealing with marabunta stings long enough to know that they were not life threatening.

At school we would notice a puzzling phenomenon every now and then, among the pupils. A child would sometimes come to school with a perfect red oval hole at the tip of the nose or the tip of the big toe. None of the Amerindian natives seemed particularly concerned, but it worried Sister Enid and Brother Edward. The teachers explained that the bites were from bats, vampire bats that is, and since most of the natives slept in hammocks the nose and big toe were the easiest spot for the bats to access since they were often exposed. No one expressed any concern about rabies, all a bat-bite did was leave a hole that healed after a while. I have not known any of the children to develop an infected bite.

On one of his visits, I overheard Doc having a conversation with Brother Edward about vampire bats. He said that they used their noses to detect heat from a warm spot, which lead them to animals or humans. The bats preferred larger animals such as cattle, but they did not discriminate when it came to feasting. Substances in the bat's saliva would numb the spot and prevent blood from clotting, so that the victims would continue to sleep while the bats drank a full meal of their blood. I was very thankful that we had mosquito nets, or in this case, bat nets.

Then there was the dreaded piranha, called pirai (peer-eye) by the locals. Horror tales of piranha led me to expect a huge menacing fish, but the ones I saw belied that image. They were about eight to ten inches long and six inches wide. Unlike larger predators like sharks that could kill their victims quickly, piranha remind me of the saying "being pecked to death by ducks"; in this case it would be nibbled to death by sharp toothed fish. Fortunately, they are supposed to prefer dead mammals to feed on rather than the breathing kind. And if times are tough and food is scarce, instead of seeking out humans, they just eat each other, weakest one goes first. Because of this, I think that the ones people encounter would be the fittest and strongest. Not a comforting thought but it is good to be forewarned.

One of the first lessons we were taught about pirai was that they are attracted to splashing, noise, and blood. We were warned against going in the river mainly because of fear of drowning since none of us could swim and being warned about pirai was supposed to be an added deterrent. It did not work. Once our friends, who were skilled at rowing canoes at an early age, and could swim, invited us along we went, forgetting all warnings.

The few times I saw pirai was when someone cleaned fish by the riverside. Several would gather, attracted by the blood. They looked unimpressive until they opened their mouths and bared their lethal teeth. The river was the primary source of water for the village, and it served as the place to clean large cookware, do laundry, fetch water from, and bathe. Bathers would wash naked directly in the water, despite the threat of piranha.

Considering the amount of activity that took place in the river we were aware of only one instance of serious injury from piranha. Most bites took part of a finger or a toe, nothing very dramatic, but it was different for Caleb whom we never saw without footwear. Caleb served as the reference point when Sister Enid warned us of the danger of piranha, since she did not know of anyone when she was a child in Skeldon who was bitten by this fish. But Caleb did not die, and he could do everything we could, and we never saw his feet, so this example had little effect in scaring us.

Chapter 33
Pets

If you saw a cat or dog in Orealla it was guaranteed to be a stray. The only pets we knew of there were birds. Birds may not be cuddly, but their food was easy to obtain in that environment and it was free. And birds were not interested in human food. The macaws, parrots and toucans did not need cages either. This could be because their wings were clipped. Their habitat was limited to their favorite perch or pole and the open house. The birds became so tame that they would readily hop on a stick that was offered or take someone's hand or shoulder.

The absence of pets like cats and dogs was not unique to Orealla. While I lived in Guyana, the only person I heard of who had an actual pet was the wife of a physician who practiced in Port Mourant. She would often drive around with her little dog in her car. She was also the only woman I knew of who drove a car in our area. The doctor and his family lived in New Amsterdam, a larger town, and maybe they had veterinarians there, and maybe the large foreign stores stocked special pet foods. I cannot say for sure because this was not something people even considered in the places where I lived.

Having a pet was a matter of economics for most people. Feeding and taking care of the family was the priority and paying special attention to the needs of animals was not affordable. Every dog or cat we ever had showed up as a stray and someone fed it. Then it stayed forever, happy to eat the scraps from our table. In some families where even table scraps were scarce, they would often cook "fine rice" specially for dogs or cats. This type of rice consisted of the smallest pieces of the rice grain that had no value as human food (although families would use this in times of great need), and cost little. Nature might have intended for dogs and cats to be carnivores, but hunger compelled them to be otherwise.

The presence of cats meant that our food had to be put out of reach in locked cupboards or in the fridge until we were ready to eat it. Even though the animals lived outside cats were known to go to great lengths to get a piece of fish. Some homes had a very efficient method of keeping cats away from their food. Long hooks were anchored in the ceiling beams and baskets of fried fish, shrimp and other cat favorites were suspended from these. Very few people had refrigerators, even on the coast, so this method of storing food was common. It was also a very effective way of keeping treats away from children.

When the grey cat showed up one day at our door in Orealla, it got a scrap of food and no one shooed it, so it stayed. It may have been attracted by mice for every so often a litter of tiny pink mice would show up in a box where we stored clothes. This did not happen after the cat came. Grey Cat soon had a litter of kittens, all of whom eventually disappeared except for Black Cat. Black Cat later gave birth to a litter, but she was less capable of birthing than her mother. Whereas we would not even know that Grey Cat had given birth until we saw the kittens, Black Cat appeared confused by the whole process and roamed the house wailing as she gave birth. Not many of the kittens from either cat stayed around long. I did not want to think of what their fate could have been.

Once, when we were playing by the river, Tucko caught a baby water turtle that she wanted to keep. Her family did not have any sizeable containers at home that they could spare but we had a large glass jug at the bottom of our house. We did not use the jug because part of the rim was broken off and left a sharp edge. Both families agreed that the turtle could live there if we were careful with the jug and took good care of the turtle. We kept our part of the bargain and the turtle thrived. We changed its water and fed it leaves, fruit and worms. Everything was going well until the day Tucko slipped on the wet ground and her neck landed on the broken section of the jar. The adults heard our screams and rushed to the scene. The cut may have been minor because it soon healed with local treatment, but the trauma of seeing the blood stain the water and the ground, and Tucko's anguished face and screams, stayed with me for a long time.

The turtle had grown enough to be deemed capable of surviving on its own, so it was released back into the river and the jug disappeared from under the house.

Chapter 34
Native Crafts

There are two mats in my stack of hot pads that I use only on special occasions. They are tibisiri mats that we brought from Orealla in 1966, more than a half century ago. The mats are the original tan color of the tibisiri straw with blue designs painted on. They are still beautiful and show no signs of wear and tear or peeling paint.

Tibisiri is harvested from the ite palm and after processing, the pliable straw-like material is woven, mostly by women, into works of art such as mats, fans, small decorative baskets, and various trinkets.

Quakes, the large baskets that are used for transporting cassava or root vegetables from the farms, are made from various palms or reeds, as are other storage baskets and the matapee and fans that are used in baking cassava bread. These tools are created from local sources using the same natural materials and methods that the Amerindians have been using for ages.

Hammocks, that the natives use to sleep in, are also woven using traditional methods. Every aspect of hammock-making is done from scratch. Most homes have their own hand-made looms, and the cotton for making the hammocks is picked by hand from the tree, washed and treated, then spun into thread which is stored on hand-made wooden spools. If colors are introduced the thread is dyed by hand.

Since hammocks are used in place of beds, keeping this craft alive is crucial to preserving the ages-old lifestyle of the Amerindians. It is a tedious process. We watched Mama, Errol's mother, labor for months to create a hammock. It was a chore that was scheduled around her other duties. Mama's hands would fly in and out of the loom with such speed that her actions seemed automatic. It belied the knowledge and concentration that it took to create a perfect product. When we left Orealla our family was gifted with an elaborately woven hammock. It was decorated with a lacey fringe on the sides that was edged with colorful balls of dyed cotton. It was the most beautiful hammock that I had ever seen, and it was all hand made with love.

The chalk in the hills provided unlimited material for creating sculptures. In the front of the fourth standard in school, there was a shelf that spanned the width of the schoolhouse. It boasted carvings of pure white chalk made by villagers and students. Most were of animals, even animals the natives had never seen such as elephants and whales, but there were also replicas of the church and school, a bell, and a car, among others. The display changed every so often to showcase the creations of all the artists who contributed their work. Carving chalk may have been the only craft that was done purely for the artistry and pleasure of the effort.

Calabash trees provided the gourds from which eating and drinking utensils and other kitchenware were made. Both the fruit and dishes are called calabash. Several times we watched Errol's father slice a round green gourd in half, scoop out the soft white pulp with black seeds, polish the shell and leave it in the sun to dry. Depending on the size of the fruit and the cut, several types of dishes could be made. A crossway cut of a large gourd would give deep bowls for eating, and cutting a more oval calabash along the length would provide a shallow vessel for scooping. Smaller fruit were used for cups and trimming off just the top of one of the larger calabashes would create a water storage goblet. Spoons of varying sizes were also made from the gourd. Roy and I once made our own cups under the direction of Errol's father. He cut some small gourds in half and gave us and his children one half each to scoop out and smooth the insides. We let them dry in the sun like he did and soon we had our own calabash cups.

The natives of Orealla also made their own dugout canoes, along with the paddles that they used to row them. Most of the natives called these vessels corials (cu-ree-al) instead of canoes. We were able to watch Errol's father carve a corial out of a tree trunk by their waterside. In Orealla, every family had their own waterside, a portion of the riverbank that was cleared and had a path down to the riverbed below. Some families had a little jetty built in their space. It was the spot where families would go to fetch water, do laundry, bathe, clean fish and moor their corials.

Errol's family's waterside was next to ours. One day a tree trunk appeared by their waterside. We did not see how it got there but we watched Errol's father chip away at the trunk each day for what may have been weeks. He removed the bark then hacked out a hollow in the median. Errol and Tucko informed us that the tree was kabucalli, and the pride in their voices indicated that this must be a superior type of wood and that this canoe would be a premium specimen.

We were taken aback one morning when we noticed that there was a fire in the tree trunk, in the area that was hollowed out. Our alarm must have been evident, so our friends assured us that this was just how a corial was made. Apparently controlled burning helped quicken the hollowing out process. After many days, the burning ended, and the trunk was left to cool before hand tools were used to scrape out the charred wood. The form of the canoe was taking shape. Errol's father shaped, cleaned, and sanded the vessel. Seats were added, and paddles carved. The corial was finished and ready for the water.

The only tools I saw being used in the making of the canoe were hand tools perhaps a chisel, hammer, and small axe. Measurements were made by string and chalk; I saw no rulers or tape measures. Throughout the process I noticed that Errol's father worked alone, until it was time to launch the canoe. Then several men came, placed some skinny poles across the path and rolled the canoe into the water.

It was a success. It floated gracefully. There was no doubt that it would.

Chapter 35
Child's Play

All the children played enta-hole. In Orealla this was a game that was similar to marbles, but instead of the store-bought glass orbs we used the seeds of the awara fruit which were called banga. Awara seeds are about an inch in diameter and have a hard, black shell housing a dense kernel. They remind me of miniature coconuts, but unlike coconuts, the stringy covering over the seed is bright orange, juicy, and delicious. Best of all the seeds were free and a pleasure to source.

One grassless section of the schoolyard was dotted with holes for this game; three holes were dug in a straight line and were placed equal distances apart. The object of the game was to roll one's banga into all three holes in succession and reach the third hole first. If you missed rolling your game piece into a hole it stayed where it landed and that left it open to be hit farther away by the other players. Hitting the opponents' bangas as far away from the holes as possible helped one advance quicker. The best bangas were the ones that were heavy with the contents of the seed still intact. The heavier seeds allowed greater control when rolling them into the holes and they could send the opponent's banga flying when hit. Shape was also important, for a round, smooth banga rolled easier. Since nature did not guarantee a perfectly round seed in every fruit, once a perfect banga was found it was treasured and carefully guarded. However, every seed would eventually break from the constant battering they received during games. Then we would just have to eat a lot of wara to find another good one.

Skip, or jump rope, was popular among girls. Our skipping ropes were just that, lengths of rope tied at the ends that we turned and sang rhymes as we did so. We also played hopscotch, and a few variations of it such as kick seed and sal pass.

Occasionally teachers would supervise our games. Ring games seemed to be their favorite and "Colored Girl in the Ring" was one of their frequent choices. The ring consisted of as many pupils as they could round up, and this particular song had many verses. This meant that only a few children would have a turn in the ring before it was time to return to class. I found it tedious because most of us just walked around in a circle singing "There's a Colored Girl in the Ring, Tra-la-la-la-la..." over and over again. That is why I could sympathize with Huckleberry Finn when he felt that heaven was not the place for him to be if the chief form of entertainment was angels walking around singing songs. Even when games like bottle and kerchief were supervised, they lacked the edge of excitement felt when we played by ourselves. Students were prone to be less aggressive when teachers were around. The teachers' actions may have been their attempts to include everyone in games, but we did not realize that then.

Tag, in its many forms was an eternal favorite. There was 'ketcha' or catch, which was the simplest form, and bottle and kerchief, where a soft drink bottle with a handkerchief, or any old rag, draped over the top was placed in the middle of a circle of children. Two players would be chosen, and the aim was to get the kerchief off the bottle without causing the bottle to tip over or being tagged by the other player before you returned to your place in the circle. Of all the variations of tag my favorite was Watamama.

Watamama was a terror figure of local legend. From what our friends told us she was a frightening mermaid who would catch and eat children. Her lair lay deep under the river and was littered with the bones of her victims. The idea of trying to flee from a horrifying menace rather than a friend who is trying to tag you added a layer of danger and excitement to the game. We would taunt watamama with sing-song phrases like "watamama can't catch me" or "watamama going to starve today" that we chanted over and over. Our chants were accompanied by mocking gestures. Even though the game was great fun when played in the schoolyard, my favorite spot for playing watamama was the clearing under the almond tree by our waterside. This setting was more authentic for an evil sea creature to pounce upon unsuspecting children.

Most of the games we played only required readily available materials that we used to create toys. Seeds and stones, bottles and ropes were repurposed into playthings. Some homemade toys, such as slingshots, which we all learned to make from forked branches and pieces of rubber, were not allowed at school, but we did use them to fell fruit from higher branches.

The only store-bought toys I remember having during our time in Orealla were those I received for Christmas. At first, I was given dolls, but I soon found out that dolls were not as much fun as playing shoot-em-up with the boys. The hair of every doll was usually irreversibly tangled or gone by day two, so after a while I received a gun like my nephews did. The guns were made of metal and used strips of red, blue or yellow paper shots. The paper strips had tiny pockets of explosive powder along the length. When the hammer of the pistol hit one of these pockets it made a loud sound and the paper strip advanced to the next pocket of gray powder. These worked well if the powder was dry, but the humidity of the tropics quickly made them too moist to fire well. But that did not stop us from enjoying the toys; shouting "pow, pow" as a substitute for the sound of the powder worked just fine.

Chapter 36
Wrapping Up

Sports day was the most anticipated event held towards the end of the school year. The entire school body would be divided up into teams, usually four, with the uninspired names of House A, B, C and D. For weeks before, teams would practice running, relay, long jump, high jump, three-legged race, egg-and-spoon, (small rocks were used for eggs until Sports Day), and sack race. Some games such as the cali eating contest were less likely to be practiced at school. Staff members who were not associated with a House supervised and judged the contests.

The cali eating contest was a crowd favorite. Equal pieces of cassava bread would be spread with hot pepper sauce. Very hot pepper sauce. These were tied with string and hung along a strong twine which was tied between two trees. The pieces of cali would be positioned at equal distances apart to allow room for participants to maneuver. Players would stand in front of a piece of cali with their hands behind their backs until the word "go". Their goal was to finish the piece of bread as fast as they could using only their mouths. This was no easy task since the dangling bread moved with each touch of the mouth, and once you bit off a piece you had to get it into your mouth without having any fall to the ground. If any fell it counted against you. The added challenge was to survive the heat of the pepper sauce. The rule was that players were only allowed a drink of water when they had finished the game or given up, and bowls of water were placed temptingly on a table before the contestants, daring them to drink. The most memorable winner of the cali-eating contest was Leonard. Leonard dropped a piece of bread as he tried to get it into his mouth but that did not deter him; he got to his knees, hands still behind his back, downed his head, and plucked that bread with his teeth right out of the sand and finished it. He received the greatest applause that day.

The days-long celebrations included recitations and singing. On one occasion Patricia, called Pato, was chosen to recite the poem, "In the Heart of a Seed". For some unknown reason Pato could not help giggling after the first line. She tried several times with the same result, but she finally pulled herself together and finished the poem. She had the audience laughing along with her and that broke the initial silence of the attendees and encouraged their engagement.

The one song that was sung at every celebration was a traditional Amerindian song. It was usually accompanied by a gentle swaying dance called the mari-mari, and the soft sounds of the shak-shak, or maracas made from the gourds of the calabash tree. I have never seen the song in written form, and do not know if a written copy exists or if it is just passed down orally, but the Arawak words sounded like:

Beekey duma say, danda kooba tay,
Ten men a wak aroo, tu raja banday,
Dafo youfa cana say, dashee quaba naro,
Ta na na na na na, ta na na na na na
Ta na na na na na

Beewai say he aroo, dashee shaku bah,
Ten men a wak aroo, tu raja banday,
Dafo youfa cana say, dashee quaba naro,
Ta na na na na na, tan na na na na na
Ta na na na na na

I apologize to the Amerindians of Orealla if these words are off the mark.

One year I was part of the team that recited the alphabet. Each letter represented something of Amerindian or

Guyanese origin of value and a sentence or two gave information on it. I fell in love with the letter G, and to this day I remember that "G is for greenheart, the hard wood that defies both ocean and time". I practiced and perfected my delivery and asked Brother Edward to let me recite G. This did not go my way. Since I was the shortest pupil who would recite, and since they arranged the group by height, I was given Z. I was not thrilled, but I memorized Z and did my part. I do not remember what Z stood for in that recitation. I just know that it was not zed for Zebedee as the nuns had taught me in kindergarten.

Classroom furniture was scrubbed at the end of each school year. All desks and benches were taken out into the school yard and washed with soap and water and stiff brushes. Pupils in third and fourth standard did the scrubbing, while the younger children dried with squares of old rags. The furniture was left outside until dismissal to get the full benefit of solar drying power. One desk had the initials R.H.E.C. carved so deeply into it that even after years of scrubbing those letters remained engraved in the wood. They stood out because of the ink that had seeped into the hollows and stained the letters.

Treats were often the highlight of each of these days. Besides the usual milk and biscuits, we received Kool-Aid and the kind of biscuits that had white or lemon cream in them, and hard candies which looked like jewels.

Chapter 37
Father Come

Every two to three months or so Father and Mrs. Tatnall would come to Orealla to see to the affairs of the church and to conduct mass, baptisms, and weddings. Their visit was a big deal.

    The house that we occupied was assigned for the use of the priest on his visits, and the dedicated headmaster's house was the one next door which we called Mr. James' house, since he had lived there at one time. Because Mr. James' house was not in the best shape an agreement was reached. The headmaster and his family were permitted to live in the priest's house in exchange for accommodating the priest and his wife and tending to their needs during their visits. This meant that whenever Father and Mrs. Tatnall came, we had to move over to the house next door.

    Sister Enid, Delia and other temporary helpers cleaned and scrubbed Mr. James' house before the visit. It was a chore for the adults but an adventure for us children. We only brought over whatever clothing and necessities we needed for the duration of the visit, usually a week or less. Our beds stayed at the other house, and we slept on a huge ground bed on the newly scrubbed floor. The Tatnalls would usually bring us books and they were not all religion based. The first time we read *The Saggy Baggy Elephant* and *Little Black Sambo* was by the light of a handlamp on that very ground bed.

    Meals were prepared at the priest's house and brought over to us. We did not eat with the company. As far as I remember, the dining room table was used for eating only by Brother Edward, and the priest and his wife when they visited; the books and papers that normally covered the surface were packed away neatly on the bookshelf, and a white, hand-embroidered tablecloth was laid.

Meal presentation was a little more elaborate in honor of the guests. There would be fresh sliced tomatoes and lettuce, newly arrived on the boat that brought the guests, and even a fancy dessert – usually Jello or a can of mixed fruit in heavy syrup, served with Nestle's Clotted Cream that came in a can all the way from Devonshire, England. Although these were good, the premium dessert for us children came from an industrial sized tin of Peek Frean Biscuits. Peek Frean and Co. made biscuits by appointment to Her Majesty, The Queen, so you knew they had to be good. We got to choose two biscuits (cookies) each from the can about once per week. The ones with cream always went first.

Education was a top priority for the missionaries who visited Orealla long before, and they successfully brought English and Christianity to the mission. None of my classmates knew their native language, and only the older adults could speak it but rarely did so. We all communicated in Creolese, the dialect that is common throughout the country. Even though the English language is its core, the pronunciation of words in Creolese has evolved in a manner that is unique to Guyana and the British West Indies. The addition of Hindi words and some of African origin give the dialect a unique spin.

Since the comforts that the Tatnalls were accustomed to were not available in Orealla, Sister Enid and Brother Edward did what they could to help make their stay more endurable. Sister Enid would heat great pots of water on the stove so that they could have a warm bath. The fine porcelain dinnerware, which we called "ware" plates, would be brought out and knives and forks and hand embroidered serviettes would be set at the table. At that time, we never used knives and forks, and rarely spoons, for our fingers took care of all our feeding needs. In fact, one was liable to be accused of putting on airs and being "English fi" if they used these table utensils in Guyana then. No one wanted to be labeled pretentious.

The only time the teapot and teacups were used was when the Tatnall's visited. These were placed on a silver tray and Father and Mrs. Tatnall would pour their tea and add as much sugar and Carnation milk as they wanted. Our tea was brewed in a pot on the stove and milk and sugar were added to the pot before the tea was served to us. I did not mind. I loved the tea the way it was prepared, strong, with milk and sugar. We used raw, brown, Demerara sugar. The Tatnalls, being our guests, were served the fancy white sugar, Tate and Lyle brand, that came all the way from England. I never could have guessed at that time that it was us who were using the good stuff, the raw, brown sugar. It took a few decades, and a movement that favors less processed foods that made me realize that.

As to the matter of the outhouse, it received a thorough scrubbing with liberal amounts of Jeyes fluid, and the Tatnall's got to use real toilet paper every time. They would be given several rolls and would visit the outhouse, roll in hand. There would be a spare that hung on a long nail just in case one was to accidentally drop a whole roll into the cavity. We took advantage of the liberal offering of the spare roll during this time and shunned the squares of newspaper that were stuck to another nail.

It took me a long while to notice that outhouses existed only in the back yards of the non-natives. I had never seen one elsewhere, so it made me wonder about how Amerindians took care of their outhouse needs. One day while we were playing Tucko suddenly got up, went into the bushes, and came back within minutes. I suspected what might have happened, but I needed confirmation. This was too serious a subject for me to have to guess at. Tucko revealed that a hole was dug for obvious purposes and then covered over. Since the area was sandy this was an easy task. I must have asked for the full picture because I was told why leaves were necessary during such activity. Since they would never need toilet paper with the abundance of leaves around, I was glad that Tucko and her family would never have to hear any snarky comments from the clerk at J.P. Santos on the reason why we needed so much toilet paper. On the other hand, I was uncomfortable with the notion of her squatting in a place that was filled with venomous snakes and stinging insects. I tried not to think of what one would have to do if there was a bite or sting in the middle of nature's call.

Chapter 38
That Part of Life Called Death

Children were not sheltered from death. Not in Oreallla, nor elsewhere in Guyana. Death was part of the tapestry of their lives. Many watched their grandparents lying sick in bed, dying long before the day that bodily death came. They were aware of the many newborn children, often their brothers or sisters, who perished before they had a chance to be known and loved and properly mourned. But these deaths were common enough to not generate the kind of shock or anguish that unexpected dying had the power to cause.

My mother's death was the first I suffered, but at age two I could not remember it. I have a better memory of my father's passing, but the scenes and emotions are vague.

The first death that I clearly recall (except for chickens being butchered), was when the cow died in Oreallla. I do not remember many cows in the village but the memory of this cow remains fresh because of the manner in which it died. The animal had wandered over to a home on cassava bread baking day and had drunk from the bowl of cyanide tainted cassava juice that was squeezed out of the matapee. By the time someone noticed, the cow had consumed a lethal dose.

We became aware of what had happened when we saw a crowd gathering in the field in front of Mr. Julius' shop. The cow lay on the grass foaming at the mouth, struggling for breath and twitching all over, but it was the groans that unnerved me most. Shaken, I hurried home before the end came. I heard that someone had shot the cow to end its misery sooner. It was a long time before I could look at that field and not have that scene replay in my mind.

One night I had a dream of a white bird, it looked like a dove from pictures I had seen of doves. The bird flew over our house three times then flew straight up into the heavens. I awoke with the sure knowledge that my grandfather had died. I did not hear voices or receive any specific message from beyond. I just knew. A few hours later we got the news from the district commissioner that Aja had indeed died. The district officer granted permission for Sister Enid and me to ride in the speedboat, the Macusi, on an emergency basis to go to Skeldon for the funeral.

Aja's body was laid out in his house where the wake and prayer services were held. Ladies made tea by the gallon with milk and sugar. The tea and buttered Edger Boy biscuits, and homemade snacks, were served to the mourners. The crowd of attendees covered the front yard, the bridge in front of the house, and spilled out into the street. After the wake, arrangements were made for the body to be transported to Number 63 Beach on the Atlantic shore for cremation, and for his ashes to be scattered into flowing water.

The custom was that the coffin would be placed in a truck with the music of traditional Indian instruments accompanying the singing of bajans, or Hindu religious songs, by a bevy of ladies. It was my grandfather's specific wish that this was how he should be taken to the cremation site. The family did not observe his request. Since some family members had become well off, they wanted my grandfather to have an upper class send off, so they laid the coffin in a hearse. The hearse was driven for about a mile, then it sputtered and died. The driver got out and examined the engine and all seemed well, so he started it again. After a couple of miles, the same happened. Experienced mechanics could find nothing wrong with the hearse. After one more try with the same results the coffin was placed in the truck with the music and singing ladies. The truck ran fine, and so did the same hearse that gave problems earlier.

I am a firm believer in science. I have worked in the medical field for many years, but I also know that we have not solved all the mysteries of the universe yet. Science may someday have an explanation for everything, but as of now there are many occurrences that we cannot easily explain.

I was in the front row before the funeral pyre and watched in awe as a piece of wood fell and crushed Aja's burning skull. I loved my grandfather dearly and was incredibly sad, but the next morning when the ladies looked for footprints in the covered tray of flour that they had laid out the night before, there were none. Any type of footprint would have indicated that Aja was reincarnated as that animal, but since there were none, it meant that he had ended the cycle of reincarnation, achieved moksha, and was now one with God. There was no reason to be sad.

My first encounter with murder was more traumatic than the death of the cow even though I never saw the victims in the flesh. At seven or eight years of age, one does not easily forget a parade of bodies, covered in white sheets, passing by just feet away. We were able to get a close-up look because all the adults in the house, like most of the village, had congregated by the stelling to watch the murdered remains of three men come in. Makeshift gurneys were used to transport the dead from the river to the church where the bodies were held until the authorities arrived to take them to the coast. Our house stood along the path to the church, and we joined the onlookers that lined up on each side.

We heard snippets of what transpired by being quiet and invisible. The adults tried to speak in low tones, but such news did not lend itself to whispers. As the story goes, four men from the coast had come to Orealla with a large sum of money to do business, most likely to purchase logs, but one wanted to keep that money. The men had come by private boat, so it was just the four of them on board when the murders took place. The one who plotted the burglary and murder convinced one of the others to join him and split the proceeds. After using a cutlass to butcher, or chop up as it was termed, the sleeping men, the plotter killed his accomplice, sank the boat with the bodies in it and escaped with the loot. The murderer must have thought that since the bodies sank with the boat, they would remain hidden, but he did not take into account that gas build up during decomposition would cause them to eventually float to the surface. The bodies of the men were found floating on the river days later and brought to Orealla, the nearest settlement.

The story made the national news. The murderer cooked up some implausible tale that was full of holes. He was tried in court, and after several appeals and retrials by some of the leading barristers in Guyana, he was found guilty, sentenced to death, and executed.

I later learned that the perpetrator was caught because he asked a friend to collect the money which he had buried under a marked tree on an island in the river. *6 The friend went to the police and assisted them in extracting a confession from the murderer. Even though the murderer confessed some of the lawyers still attempted to free him on technicalities but they ultimately failed. *6

Our family had at least two close calls in the river. One day Joshua and I were playing in the shallows by the shore when he started to wander into the water. I called after him, but he just kept going forward. In a panic I ran to get Sister Enid. I could barely get the words out, but my gestures told her what was happening. She raced to the riverside, grabbed Joshua, and pulled him to safety.

Then there was the incident with me. I was playing alone on the jetty at our waterside one day with my assortment of treasures; mora seeds, smooth stones, and a few sticks which I used to pry open the mora seeds. I was too absorbed in my play to notice that the tide had come in and that the water was lapping at the jetty. I knew it was not safe to stay there at high tide, so I got up to head home. In my haste I slipped on a mora seed and fell into the water.

The next thing I remember was that I was being pulled out of the river by my hair. My nephew Paschal, who was home for the holidays, did not see or hear me fall, but he saw my hair spread out upon the water and pulled me on to the jetty. I will always be grateful to Paschal for saving my life that day. What has always puzzled me was that I did not struggle even though I could not swim. I remember just bobbing peacefully in the water. It may have been mere seconds, but those seconds left an indelible imprint on my mind. It was not my time; I was saved for a reason. There is a deeper meaning in there somewhere.

Chapter 39
Chocolates from Heaven

Without warning, at least for us children, a squad of dark green helicopters landed in the field near Mr. Julius' shop one day. They carried white soldiers who moved into Mr. James' house.

The soldiers set to work right away, fixing the stairs, and making other repairs in the house. Better yet, they dug a well and fitted it with a hand pump. In a matter of hours, at the side of the house, a working water pump stood. We watched as the first pumps spit out muddy water to great applause. It was the first standpipe in the village. Before that we used rainwater that collected in steel drums that originally held oil. If our rainwater ran low, we would resort to using water from the river for laundry or bathing. All water used for cooking or drinking was boiled for several minutes since water borne illnesses were a concern. The boiled water was stored in a covered white bucket in the kitchen, or in bottles in the fridge. Remi developed typhoid fever at one point but thankfully, he recovered under his mother's care.

The best part of the soldier's visit were the bars of chocolates they tossed at us. There would always be a gawking crowd at the house since it was not every day that one saw white men and helicopters and such. Maybe the soldiers felt that we would take the chocolate bars, share them, and leave, but it had the opposite effect. More children came. No one asked for anything, we all just stood there looking at the strangers and then it rained chocolate bars.

Our questions about the presence of the soldiers were never answered. None of us children knew what was going on until much later when we learned that there were racially and politically motivated riots on the coast and that the adults were trying to protect us from such upsetting news. Thankfully, the fighting did not come our way. The adults were successful in keeping the frightening news from us for we had no inkling of the troubles elsewhere in the country so when others spoke of "the riots" everyone but us understood what that felt like.

Confrontations between the two major races, East Indian and African, were not uncommon but the riots of 1964-1965 were more violent than usual and were spreading throughout the country. Given that Guyana was then a British colony, soldiers from England were dispatched to help quell the violence. The squad in Orealla must have been sent to be at the ready in case of trouble in Orealla or the neighboring coastal towns of Skeldon, Springlands, and Crabwood Creek.

Sister Enid prepared dinner for the soldiers one evening and it was delivered to their house. She made curried fish, rice and roti, an East Indian flatbread. Two senior soldiers came over the next day and asked about making roti. Since the bread is made with just four ingredients, flour, baking powder, oil, and water, and is cooked on a griddle instead of an oven, it would be a good recipe to have in times of limited resources, so Sister Enid demonstrated the process. Not surprisingly, the officers called the roti tea cakes.

The soldiers seemed to enjoy their time in Orealla. Besides digging the well, they made many repairs to Mr. James' house and gave children helicopter rides. I was not one of the lucky ones chosen to ride. They also loved to frolic in the river but sadly, that did not end up so well for one of the soldiers. He hurt his neck while diving and a helicopter took him away. We heard whispers that he might have been paralyzed. I hoped that that was not the case.

Just as suddenly as they had arrived, the soldiers one day packed up and flew away.

Chapter 40
Holy Cow

Sister Enid tried to vary the menu when the priest and his wife visited. Chicken and fish sent from the coast were staples, and if she could procure some local fish from the villagers that helped change meals up a little, but one could not count on a regular supply of fish from the village. And so, Sister Enid decided to try cooking beef. She knew the Tatnalls ate beef so the next boat that brought them also brought us some steamed chunks of beef from Brother Maywah and Sister Marge.

Sister Enid was brought up in a strict Hindu household where no one ate beef since the cow was considered sacred. My grandfather had never eaten any type of meat or eggs, and although he drank milk and had other dairy products, he avoided leather goods. He wore wooden shoes called karow at home. Sister Pat and Sister Judy made cakes without eggs specially for Aja on holidays. Unlike Sister Enid, my brothers were not too particular about what foods the family traditions forbade. They had friends of different races and they all enjoyed a variety of food at each other's homes, including beef.

Sister Enid had reasoned that it was alright for the family to eat beef since everyone was Christian, and I was on my way to being confirmed. However, although she was comfortable with the rest of us eating beef, Sister Enid did not plan on having any herself. The taboos of her Hindu childhood upbringing still held fast even though she was now Christian.

The beef was curried. In fact, I think everything can be curried. But now Sister Enid had a dilemma. Since she, like every Guyanese cook I know, did not measure ingredients there was no way to tell if the curry had enough salt or garam masala or pepper unless she tasted it. She took a spoonful of gravy, cooled it, and poured it into her palm to taste. She thought it was good but felt compelled to spit it out and gargle the sin away. The priest and his wife and the rest of us all enjoyed the dish, but I do not think that we, the children, were told that we were eating beef the first few times. Not that it would have mattered. For us it was meat and it tasted good, and it did not give us kinna and that was that.

Living in Orealla made us try different foods that we normally would not eat. Unscaled fish, such as lau lau and others in the catfish family, was frowned upon and considered undesirable as they were bottom feeders, but sometimes we had that for dinner with the skin removed. The Tatnalls did not care, the Amerindians did not care, and neither did we.

It seemed unfair to me that a fish should be judged as good for eating by whether it has scales or not. The cannibalistic, man-eating piranha is covered from gill to tail with scales, yet I would have to be in a state of desperation to dig into a piranha.

You would think that someone who tried the dreaded powis, and unscaled fish would not have a problem eating beef, but Sister Enid needed to proceed slowly. Curried beef was usually cooked with potatoes, so Sister Enid just nibbled at the potatoes at first until she no longer felt the urge to spit them out. After chewing and spitting out the beef a few times she managed to swallow a bit without choking. But she had a stomachache the rest of that day and all night. There were no physical symptoms, she said, just an ill feeling. Eventually she was able to keep down the beef and has been enjoying it ever since.

Chapter 41
Catch of the Day

The boys were planning to go fishing. They did not want me to know but I had overheard them whispering about going and so I kept following them foot to foot, ignoring their orders to go away. They finally accepted that I was going to be part of their fishing group whether I was welcome or not and they soon became tired of shooing me. They pointedly ignored me instead, but I kept trailing behind. I knew, and they knew, that it was not a good idea to protest too loudly and cause a scene because then everyone would be banned from going.

I was especially determined to go with them that day because when they spoke of fishing I looked up at the heavens and saw a sign. A sure sign. The clouds had formed a pattern of overlapping scales. The fish would bite today. As a child in Skeldon Sister Enid had known plenty of fishermen who would check the clouds before setting off to fish, and who became excited when the clouds looked like that. Especially Uncle Benny. And the sign never failed; he always brought home fish and crab bucketful by bucketful on days like that. I had never caught a fish but the sky assured me that my luck was about to change.

First, we had to see to our fishing rods. They were no more than lengths of bamboo or a long skinny branch with string tied to one end, and a homemade hook made from a safety pin secured on the string. The last time we had tried fishing we had thrown the rods under the house in frustration at our lack of success and now there was a tangled mess to unravel. After straightening out the strings and checking the hooks, we took the rods and our tin cups, which were cans that formerly held Bartlett pears in heavy syrup, to a spot where earthworms were supposed to be plentiful. The cups were to put our worms in along with a bit of moist soil to keep them alive as we fished.

My nephews tried to further dissuade me from tagging along by making sure I helped to catch the worms. I was not too keen on this, but I steeled myself and pulled at fat, pink wiggly worms and added them to the tins.

When we got to the stelling I hoped that the boys would have gracefully accepted my presence by then and help me bait my hook. No such luck. They must have observed my aversion to gathering the worms and added another element to dissuade me. They told me that when I baited the hook if I showed fear or made a face no fish would bite. But I was determined. I could not understand how the fish would know whether I was afraid or frowning, and was itching to propose the question, but I did not think it was the right time to pursue an argument on the subject. Or any subject, given the atmosphere and my audacity to include myself when I was clearly not welcome. I steadied my hook, picked up a wriggler, and closed my eyes. I baited the hook by touch. I do not recommend this method, but it worked for me. And I only had to do it once.

We sat at the stelling for what seemed like hours, but the fish were not biting. I convinced myself that I must have misread the clouds. Finally, I felt a tug on my line. There was no reel to shorten the string, so I jerked on the line to bring the fish up. My catch was small, maybe ten inches long, and skinny. I was thrilled at my success but now I was faced with another problem; I needed to get the fish off the hook. Given my nephews' demeanor that day and seeing that I was the only one who got a catch I nixed the idea to ask them for help.

I walked home with my fishing rod stretched at arm's length before me with the fish dancing at the end of it. I hoped it would not spring back with enough force to touch me. I just wanted to catch a fish, not to touch it or have it touch me. It was not a pleasant walk, but Delia rescued me.

I had a piece of the fish at dinner that night. I wish I could say it was the best fish I had ever tasted, but in today's language I would describe it as "meh".

Chapter 42
My Torn Dress

Girls did not wear pants or shorts in Orealla, or in most of Guyana at that time. Dresses and skirts were the rule, but that did not stop us from climbing trees and playing games like ketcha or walking stick. What we called walking sticks are more commonly known as stilts. Ours were homemade and often the footrest would wobble and sometimes separate from the branch it was nailed on to. Wearing a dress proved a hindrance when playing such games until I copied what Tucko did when we climbed the calabash tree in their yard. She gathered the ends of her dress between her legs and tied them in a knot. This resulted in makeshift shorts which made it easier to scale trees and save the dress from being caught in the branches. Our dresses were long and hit below the knee, so it was easy to create the "shorts". The mini skirt was not yet born.

    I was forbidden to climb the tree in the school yard. At Tucko's house there was not an audience of dozens of boys like there was at school. Sister Enid allowed my makeshift shorts at home but it would not have been seemly to tie my dress in that manner at school or to climb trees then, so the rule was laid down. I obeyed when Sister Enid was around, but when we stayed after school for extra lessons for the Common Entrance Examination, I followed my friends' lead after we were done. We climbed the tree. Brother Edward and the other teachers who stayed late were usually too busy working to notice or to care

    All went well for a while until the day my dress became caught in the branches and ripped at the seam on the waistline. I knew what awaited me at home, a few lashes but worse yet, the lecture. I began to cry. My friends gathered around me wondering why I was crying simply because my dress was ripped. I explained my fear to them.

Nelly lived close to the school, and her mother had a sewing machine, so she offered to take me home and ask her mother to help.

Nelly's mother did not answer when her daughter told her about my plight and asked her to stitch my dress. She simply told me to take it off. Right there in the open. I was eight and the only underwear I wore were homemade cotton panties, like all the girls I knew. I was self-conscious but the process did not last long and the three of us were the only ones around. Nelly's mother had bright yellow thread in her machine, and she did not change it. My patterned green and white dress was stitched with white thread so the yellow made it clear that it was ripped and restitched.

I was too relieved that my dress was repaired to worry about what would happen on wash day when Sister Enid noticed the difference in the thread. I need not have worried. She probably did not notice, or did and chose not to say anything, or Delia happened to wash that dress. Sister Enid and Delia would do the washing together with each taking random garments from those that were soaking in the tub with Fab detergent. I believe that Delia got that dress and did notice but said nothing. And maybe she covered for me by always picking that dress to wash.

Chapter 43
I Confess

It was a few months before my tenth birthday when the bishop came all the way from Georgetown, the capital city of Guyana, to perform our confirmation ceremony. There were about a dozen of us who had completed the required Bible study and were ready to become full members of the Anglican Church.

Since I was not baptized as a baby, my baptism took place the day before confirmation at the font in the church. Sister Enid and Brother Edward became my godparents, and Owah Moshe was a witness.

Before the bishop arrived, we were all instructed in proper bishop-greeting protocol. We were told that he would be wearing a big ring and that people usually kissed it. His hat was not a crown but a miter. I was familiar with the word "miter" since that was one of the words we needed to know for the Common Entrance Exam. Question: What is the hat of a bishop called? Answer: miter. The bishop was not Father, but My Lord. That last one puzzled me. It did not sound right because I thought we could only call Jesus and His Father by that title.

We were so nervous about saying or doing the wrong thing that none of us made a sound when the bishop was introduced. But then he went down the line and shook hands with us. Everyone feebly and silently shook his hand, except for me. I firmly took his hand, smacked that ring and called him *Your Highness*.

We were asked to make a list of our sins to confess to the bishop. Before confirmation is the only time that we were required to make confession in the Anglican Church. I was determined to be free of all sin after I received that blessing, so I put a lot of thought into creating my list.

As we stood in line to enter the church, the bishop passed by and tried to make small talk. He asked if we had our lists ready. Everyone held up theirs. Most lists had four or five sins. Six at the most. Mine had more than a dozen.

I was ashamed of the amount of sinning I had done compared to everyone else. It worried me more because I was sure I had forgotten some. One in particular that I chose to leave out was the fact that I was more excited to taste the communion wafer than to be fully accepted into the faith. That sacred body of God, whom only the fully initiated could receive would soon be in my hands.

When it was my turn to confess, I read out the first few sins. The really important ones. Like the time I took Irene's brand-new fountain pen without asking. I liked the shade of ink she had; it was bright blue and so much nicer than the Parker's blue-black that was the staple at our home. I just wanted to write my name in that pretty color and put back the pen. I did not ask because it was brand new, and Irene was all show-offy with it so I knew she would say no. When Irene left for the bathroom, I took the pen and hurriedly wrote my name, but then the nib broke. Irene was already on her way back. In a panic, I shoved the pen in my book bag and pretended not to hear when Irene asked where her pen was. I could not think of anything then other than if Irene knew that I broke her pen I would have to tell Sister Enid and ask her for money to pay for it. Worst of all, there would be a lecture. A long one. My plan did not work so well. Trouble was, my bookbag was made of clear plastic. Irene looked over at the growing bright blue stain on my exercise book in the bag and she knew. I had to tell my sister and ask her for money to pay for the pen. And, there was a lecture. A long one. And Irene did not speak to me for days.

I had trouble defining this sin. It was not stealing for I did not steal the pen. I did not want it. I stayed quiet when Irene asked about it, so I did not tell a lie. And I paid for it.

It was a sin because I knew what I did was wrong but there was no commandment that said, "Thou shalt not take and break thy friend's pen", or something to that effect so I had to relate the whole incident to the bishop. I was about to start on the rest of my list when I received incredible insight. Like a miracle. I asked God to forgive ALL my sins and ALL my trespasses and since he was God, he would know every bad thing I had done and forgive them all. I thanked The Lord in advance.

I think the bishop must have thanked The Lord also.

Chapter 44
Fireworks

On May 26, 1966, Guyana gained independence from England. There were countrywide celebrations and Orealla was no exception.

To mark the special event, a concert was organized where we sang patriotic songs such as Dear Land of Guyana, The Song of Guyana's Children or My Native Land, and the brand-new National Anthem, which we had practiced for weeks before.

We did not have our own books that featured these songs. Only the teacher had a book and would either read the words while we wrote them down or would write them on the blackboard for us to copy. Writing the whole song on the board was tedious so we mostly copied as he read. This is probably why, for years when I sang the chorus of The Song of Guyana's Children, instead of "Onward, upward may we ever go", I belted out "Onward, upward, Mary have a go". I could not figure out who Mary was or what she was having a go at, but I urged her on with all my might.

Wood and chalk carvings of the map of Guyana, and local arts and crafts were on display. There were also paper maps with the new name of the country, and we had to get used to saying Guyana instead of British Guiana, or BG, and learn to spell Guyana the new way.

That may have been the last term in which we had to do sums in pounds, shillings, and pence. I was not sad to see the end of that. I understood it well enough when it appeared in English literature to know that tuppence was not worth much but having to do math calculations using this currency did not come easy. We were not familiar with it since we used Guyanese money which was in the same denominations as in the U.S.A., in dollars and cents. There were one hundred cents to a dollar. However, we called a cent a cent and not a penny. A penny in Guyanese currency was a coin worth two cents and this was often called a big jil. The older folk would still refer to items as being worth a shilling or two bits and speak of gold in sovereigns and pennyweight, vestiges of an era that was long gone.

Independence Eve in Orealla was the first time any of us had seen fireworks except Sister Enid. I believe she saw them when she visited Georgetown to see Princess Margaret on her tour in 1958.

The whole village turned out for the spectacle. Parents lined up with their children along the length of the school waiting in tense anticipation to see this wonderful thing they had heard of. An area in the far end of the side yard was cleared and the district commissioner set off the fireworks.

We did not expect the volume of the explosions and we instinctively covered our ears. The sight before us, however, was breathtaking. It may be because it was the first time that I had seen fireworks, but those sparkling starbursts, rosettes and blazing streams of light in a myriad of colors exploding against a pitch-black sky, unpolluted by other lighting, remains one of the most stunning displays I have ever seen.

Chapter 45
Errol

Something was happening next door at Errol and Tucko's house. People were gathering. The kitchen door was the closest exit to get to their house, but Sister Enid and Delia were busy in there and were not likely to step away anytime soon. Sister Enid was coating chunks of fish in flour and deep frying them. Delia had her head down at the trough, putting all her might into scouring the sooty pots and pans with ashes from the fireside, to restore their shine. All the windows and door were left open to let the smell out and the bare whisper of a breeze in. The two women were not likely to be easily distracted and might not notice if I snuck out the kitchen door, but if they should happen to see me walking towards Errol's house and then saw the crowd, they would for sure call me back, and it was unwise to disobey Sister Enid. She had strong feelings about how children, especially girl children, should behave, and poking their noses in other people's business was high on the list of no-nos. Little did she know that I learned a lot about other people's business without much effort from hearing her and Delia gossip.

I had to strategize my escape to avoid being seen. The front door was my best bet. I stepped gingerly on the floorboards in my bare feet, careful to avoid the ones that squeaked, ran down the stairs, then made a dash for the church next door. I ran along the side of the building away from our house so that I would be out of sight if Sister Enid or Delia should happen to look in that direction.

The crowd had grown, and several people now formed a barrier between the cassava trough that sat just outside the hut and the low, wooden bench at the edge of the open floor. They were riveted to the spot looking down at the floor with rapt attention. Some of the women had a hand over their mouths, never a good sign. I could not see what was going on because of the mass of bodies before me, but I had the advantage of being small and wiry. Soon I had a front row view. Errol was lying on a canvas spread on the bare earthen floor. Owah Moshe, his grandfather, had his mouth to a spot near Errol's ankle. He was sucking at it and spitting out blood. Errol's father seemed to be holding on tightly to something in front of him. I assumed it was Errol's leg because of his position but his back was to me and blocked my view.

I inched my way further to the right until I was able to see Errol. His mother cradled his head in her lap as she dabbed at his face with a cloth. The look on Errol's face scared me; it was twisted in pain and had become darker, and he had a strange look in his eyes, as if he was not seeing anything even though they were open. When his mother raised his head and wiped the corner of his mouth there was a bright red spot on the cloth.

The crowd had grown and now formed a circle around the four. I was being squeezed against the bench, but I had seen enough and did not want to be there any longer. I felt sick and needed to get away, so I wiggled my way out of the crowd and headed for home. The strange knot in the middle of my stomach that threatened to empty its contents was new to me.

Delia caught up with me. She and Sister Enid had seen the crowd and had left their chores to come see what was going on. She took my hand and walked back to the house with me.

I was too caught up in watching what was happening with Errol to hear the whispers of the crowd behind me. Delia filled me in. She told me that it was a snake bite and that my sister was talking to Roy, my nephew, who was with Errol when he was bitten. The two had gone up Sand Hill to fetch branches to make stands for smoking the excess fish that Errol's father had caught that day. It was a good catch, and they were going to slowly smoke what they did not use up right away to preserve it.

As Roy told it, he and Errol had already gathered enough branches and were about to head home when they heard a strange sound. Before either boy could react, the rattlesnake struck Errol. In a panic, they tossed the branches and ran down the hill. Breathless, they tried to explain what had happened, but they did not need to say much. The family knew through experience. Owah Moshe was summoned, and he immediately began his treatment. Roy, in a state of shock, retreated to the church steps. He could see them treating Errol until the crowd blocked his view. That was where Sister Enid found him.

Delia dried my tears and assured me that all would be well, and that Errol would get better like his sister Tucko did when she suffered that bad cut on her neck. Delia had witnessed many snake bites and recoveries through her lifetime and told us that Owah Moshe and many of the elders knew what roots and leaves and tree bark were good for drawing out snake poison. They also knew special ceremonies and prayers that would help Errol recover.

That night I added my own special prayer and hoped that Delia was right. Brother Edward's tenure was up, and we were leaving Orealla for the last time in a matter of months. I did not want my memories of the village and my friend to be marred by .... I refused to say or think the word lest it come true, but I begged God to save Errol.

The day after Errol was bitten, we had a special assembly and the entire school was educated on what to do in case of a snake bite.

According to the knowledge of that time, the victim was to move as little as possible, a piece of cloth should be tied about a foot above the bite and if someone else is present they should suck out the poison. The poison would not hurt the person who suctioned it and spat it out. Tying the cloth was supposed to stop or limit the flow of poison to other

parts of the body and prevent severe tissue and organ damage. The updated directions for treating a snake bite, according to The Cleveland Clinic are as follows:
- Remove any jewelry or watches, as these could cut into the skin if swelling occurs.
- Keep the area of the bite below the heart in order to slow the spread of venom through the bloodstream.
- Remain still and calm. If you can, roll over to your side and rest in the <u>recovery position</u>. Moving around a lot will cause the venom to spread faster through the body.
- Cover the bite with a clean, dry bandage. Try to use a pressure immobilization bandage if you can. This type of bandage should be tightly wrapped around the bite. Then, wrap another bandage around the entire limb, so that it's immobilized.

Among the list of things not to do are to not apply a tourniquet, or try to suck out the poison, the opposite of what we were taught at that time. *7

As far as I am aware there was no antivenom available at the clinic in the village when the snake bit Errol.

The instructions we learned that day came too late for Roy and Errol. They panicked and ran down the hill. By the time Errol reached home at the foot of Sand Hill the poison had already circulated throughout his system. Owah Moshe must have known this but in his desperation to save his grandson he tried the suck the poison out anyway.

After a couple of days, we saw Errol being carried to an engine boat. His mother and the boat driver boarded for their trip to the coast to seek medical attention. The villagers gathered at the stelling to wish them well and many silent prayers were said. Then the boat took off and the crowd dispersed.

***

A few hours later we saw the villagers trickling towards the waterside. The residents up on chalk hill had first seen the boat on the river and made their way down, joined by others along the way. We followed the crowd to see what was happening. It was the boat that had left earlier that very day carrying Errol for treatment. Everyone knew what had happened.

Errol's mother sat softly sobbing as she cradled the covered form in her lap. We were shooed aside as many helping hands reached out to the boat. I did not see Tucko among the crowd.

We walked home to the tolling of the church bells.

Chapter 46
Goodbye

We left Orealla shortly after Errol's passing. We were headed for Port Mourant, Brother Edward's hometown on the coast where we would now live.

The village turned out to say farewell to us. They gathered at the stelling, their faces somber, as ours were. The villagers gifted Brother Edward and Sister Enid with a hand spun cotton hammock decorated with fringes and colorful balls, which they graciously accepted with tears knowing the amount of time and dedication that went into creating this gift.

Sister Enid and Brother Edward were thankful that we all survived the many dangers we faced in Orealla, especially after Errol's death, and after the headmaster who replaced Brother Edward lost a son to drowning in the Corentyne river. I did not then realize the full import of the worry that both Sister Enid and Brother Edward must have endured while we lived in Orealla, until much later.

Orealla is changing. Electricity was introduced in 2007. There is now a police station, several prepared food shops that sell non-Amerindian dishes, a radio station, telephone, and internet service. Several Christian denominations have established a base in Orealla, among them the Church of the Nazarene and that of the Jehovah's Witnesses.

There is also a fruit processing plant that creates jams and jellies from the abundant supply of fruit. These products, along with other native items such as cassareep, find a ready market in the coastal towns*8.

The village is being promoted as a destination for ecotourism and with good reason. There are virgin forests with numerous species of animals in their native habitat, varying landscapes, and unusual fish and birds. And of course, snakes.

Change is inevitable and there is no going back for Orealla. I write this to preserve my memories and to leave a record of the mission as it was in the 1960s when I lived there. Although missionaries had educated and converted the inhabitants to Christianity, and introduced western language, behaviors, and forms of dress decades before, much of the Amerindian culture was still evident when we lived in Orealla. The village was mostly unspoiled then and the lifestyle and traditions of the Amerindians made the culture unique.

As was common when the early churches established missions and introduced education in the language of the Church, the use of indigenous languages was discouraged. Since these tongues are based on oral tradition there are no written forms to refer to, so the language only survives in the spoken form among the elders. The people of Orealla would like to preserve their traditions and especially their language, but there is growing concern that the native tongue would become obsolete with the passing of the few elders who now know it. *9

The Guyanese government is trying to lead the effort to preserve the Arawak language. According to The Department of Public Information in Guyana, "the United Nations (UN) declared 2019 as International Year of Indigenous Languages, and the Indigenous Affairs Ministry is throwing its support behind the residents of Orealla-Siparuta in the perseveration of their native language." *8. This Department further states that, "the language revival was initiated by the residents (of Orealla) after a visit from linguists who researched their native tongue." This Ministry has committed to aid in the preservation of the Arawak language by providing tutors, and printing lesson books and dictionaries in Arawak. *9

I am thankful that we lived in Orealla when it still maintained many of its cultural traditions. Living in the village was a unique and unparalleled childhood experience. My memories of the village and its people are among my most treasured.

Chapter 47
Port Mourant House

Brother Edward's new posting brought us back to the coast. He was to be headmaster of the Anglican primary school in #63 Village on the Corentyne but he decided to settle his family in his bustling hometown of Port Mourant. Sister Enid loved this idea for she made it clear that she did not want to go live "behind God's back".

It was a fortunate time to be house-hunting in a sugar-estate town like Port Mourant for Guyana was then a newly independent country and the sugar estates were nationalized. The Port Mourant sugar estate had closed and the British managers left; that meant that their houses in the housing compound, which were built by the sugar estate for its administrators, were now up for sale. Brother Edward and Sister Enid were able to purchase one of those homes in the Port Mourant Compound.

The houses had different designs but there was a standard color scheme for houses in each estate. In the Port Mourant Compound the outer walls of the buildings were white, the trim and shutters were black and the zinc roofs were red. The inside was painted off-white with dark-red trim.

It was the finest house I had ever stepped in. There were gleaming hardwood floors polished to a reflective shine, all the rooms were oversized, as was the verandah off of the front door. There was a walk-in pantry and storage room that could have functioned as a small bedroom. For us, the best thing about the house was that it had indoor plumbing. There was a full bath, and sinks in the dining room and the guest room. The flush-toilet and the shower where the water poured from a shower head instead of one having to dip it from a tub, were the most welcome features. The water was still cold though.

A huge water tank collected rain water from the gutters and an electric pump forced that water up into a smaller tank at roof level for household use. However, to save electricity we still toted buckets of water up the stairs to the kitchen and reserved the water in the small tank for bathroom use.

Windows in the living and dining areas, and the kitchen faced the marketplace. Since the lot in front of the house was empty, we could easily see whether the market was bustling or not. Bustling meant that goods were plenty, the fishermen had brought in their catch, and the vegetable sellers had also arrived; it was prime time for picking up one's basket and heading off to market.

As is common in Guyana, the house was built on stilts, or on concrete posts in the case of the compound houses. There was a room built under the main floor. We are not sure whether the previous occupants used it for storage or whether it was maid's quarters. We used it for storing yard tools and implements. The rest of the bottom-house was bare, with only a jute hammock strung between two columns.

The expansive yard was fenced in and boasted a double gate. Bougainvillea, in a riot of colors, purple, red, pink and white, graced each side of the entrance. Coconut trees were later planted along the back fence and borders of zinnias in various colors, and golden marigolds outlined part of the lower level of the house.

The streets in the compound were covered in red gravel. This caused a thin layer of red dust to settle on everything, especially if the windows were open. We were thankful for the gravel in spite of the dust for it meant that we did not have to wade in ankle-deep mud every time it rained like those who lived along clay streets often had to do. And it did rain often.

Chapter 48
Electricity

The new house was well equipped with all necessities except electricity on demand. Electricity was not widely available in Guyana at that time. We purchased power from a local gentleman who owned a generator. Mr. Chun charged based upon the number of bulbs one promised to burn at the same time. Our family signed up for four bulbs burning at once.

The power came on from 5:30 to 6:30am and from 6:00 to 10:00pm. Around 9:55pm the lights would dim warning us that power would soon be cut off. Because of this power-off time we all had to be in bed by 10:00pm. I heard of my friends and classmates staying up near exams to burn the midnight oil using hand lamps but this was never the case with us. I have stayed up late many a night to finish a novel under the covers using a flashlight, but I have never done this with a text book.

To make sure his customers were honoring their promise concerning the number of bulbs they burned simultaneously, Mr. Chun would ride around on his bicycle at night and check the houses he served. If he saw that a household was burning more that they paid for her would visit the next morning with a warning that if they continued, he would start charging for the higher number of bulbs he saw them using. It was necessary for Mr. Chun to keep track in this manner for if everyone burned the lights willy nilly then the strain could be too much for the generator.

Mr. Chun allowed families to purchase electricity mainly for ironing on Sunday afternoons. This was arranged so that the generator would not be taxed in the evenings. We also used the electric pump to fill up the smaller water tank on Sundays.

The fridge was still the kerosene model we used in Orealla and Brother Edward took meticulous care of it until the boys were older and could take on this responsibility. When Sister Enid bought a gas stove it was powered by propane, and the radio still ran on batteries, so we only used electricity for lighting, ironing and to power the water pump.

Chapter 49
Primary School

We all started school later than the other pupils that year since it took some time to pack and travel back to the coast and get settled in our new home. The younger children attended St. Joseph's Anglican School. The two older boys were already students at the nearby Corentyne High School. I was placed in the Common Entrance class in preparation for writing the said exam early the next year, since I had just turned ten, the earliest age that one could sit for the exam. Being in this class meant that one was under careful scrutiny for if someone passed the exam it reflected well on the school. As a result, more effort was put into our instruction and more eyes focused on whether we were studying or not. This is where talking got me into trouble again. When I got caught, I had to stand before the teacher, stretch out my palm, and suffer the sting of lashes from a twelve-inch ruler.

I liked school. When we finished our work assignments, we were allowed to read the story books in the classroom. At St. Joseph's there was a greater selection of books and easier access to reading material than there was in Orealla. One of my favorite volumes was one on Greek mythology. The stories were as fascinating as the stories Sister Enid used to tell us.

Staying for extra lessons was a common practice for those who were to sit for the Common Entrance exam. The lessons consisted of drills in the material that was likely to appear on this test. Doing the exercises in the book of verbal reasoning was the part I liked the best, although I could not easily grasp some of the concepts like a moving sidewalk, or remember which was elevator or escalator for none of us had seen such things. Mathematics proved to be manageable for me at that level.

There were certain privileges reserved for students in this class; the boys did not have to do woodworking, and the girls were excused from cookery and sewing classes. We also did not have to sweep up the floors of our classroom at the end of the day. Academics were to be our only focus.

We wrote the exam in the spring of the next year. I was one of two who passed. We who passed were honored by having to stand on the stage at assembly and the headmaster introduced us and told the whole school of our success.

Passing this exam guaranteed me a fully funded scholarship to the preeminent school for girls in Guyana, Bishop's High School in Georgetown. But there was a problem; Georgetown was far away and we had no relatives living there. The likelihood of a girl from an East Indian family being sent to school so far away and living with strangers was almost nil. Instead, I went to Corentyne High School in nearby Rose Hall Village which was walking distance from home. I may have wanted to go to Bishop's High at that time, but I'm glad I did not get to do so. At the tender age of ten, I believe leaving the familiarity of home would have been traumatic, even if I did not experience a similar scenario five years earlier.

Chapter 50
High School

Corentyne High School, now J.C. Chandisingh Secondary School. was founded by the venerable J.C. Chandisingh in 1959. Under the watchful directorship of Mr. Chandisingh, the school had gained a reputation for being among the best secondary schools in the region, in just a few years,

The school was started in Rose Hall Village and it still is located there. School began at eight-thirty in the morning with an hour break for lunch at noon, then resumed again from one to three thirty in the afternoon.

Most of the students lived within walking distance of the school so we would walk home, have a hurried lunch, freshen up, then return to school for the afternoon session. Those who lived farther away usually came by bus and brought their food in a covered tin saucepan with a wire looped handle. When I share this, I have often been asked if the food did not spoil. The cane cutters did the same for, like the mothers of the students, their wives would cook and pack their meal early in the morning, usually rice with curried vegetables and perhaps a boiled egg or a piece of fried fish. This container would not be opened until lunchtime, hours later. I have never heard of anyone's food going bad by the time they were ready to eat it. I think that because the food was cooked fresh, then placed in the saucepan and covered immediately, there was very little likelihood of bacterial contamination until the container was opened. The same principle as canning, I imagine. Besides, as I like to say, "we Guyanese cook the daylights out of everything".

I started school in Form 1A, which was then housed in the two-story auditorium building that sat behind the main schoolhouse. Classrooms were on the lower level and the auditorium was above us. We did not need to wear school uniforms before high school, but now our navy-blue pleated skirts, white button-down shirts, navy neck tie with silver stripes, and a straw hat with a navy and silver striped ribbon around the crown, announced that we girls attended Corentyne High School. The boys wore khaki shorts, white button-down shirts and the same necktie. Boys were only allowed to wear long pants in the fifth form, regardless of height, or how skinny their legs were, in the lower forms, much to the chagrin of many.

   A few vendors sat on small benches with their wares laid out on low tables along the road close to the entrance of the school yard. These vendors did not squat on the ground with their goods before them, or sell the usual homemade treats we would find in front of other schools, such as sugar cakes or bara, or fudge. I imagine it was part of school policy to support a more hygienic food environment. These vendors instead sold hard candies and gum, though many of us had little disposable pocket money to spend freely on sweets.

   Since Guyana was a newly independent former British colony our education was still based on the syllabus outlined for students in the UK. We studied for five years, took the O Level (Ordinary Level) General Certificate of Education exams, and then those who did well enough could teach, work in a bank, or go on to Berbice High School to sit for the A level (Advanced Level) exams. Very few from our school sought the latter, for the majority of us had dreams of going abroad to study, or if not to study, to just go abroad where opportunities to build a successful life were more plentiful. Working, or going on for A levels served to fill the gap until we were approved for visas. Getting a visa could be a lengthy process for you had to have someone who lived abroad and who had a healthy bank account to sponsor you, and promise that you would not become dependent on public funds. Then you had to convince the embassy staff who interviewed you to grant you a visa. It was better if you had a close relative who could sponsor you. But all that was five years away.

Chapter 51
Clothing

Our school uniforms, and all other clothing were sewn by local tailors and seamstresses. This did not mean that we chose to have custom made clothing, it meant that we had no other choice. Ready-made clothing was not available. We longed to be able to go to a store and look through the many dresses and choose one we liked that fit us, like they did in movies. Instead, we would buy the appropriate length of cloth, go to the tailor or seamstress, have our measurements taken, and receive the finished product in a couple of weeks during slow times. The wait was double just before school started.

My regular seamstress was Meera. Meera had several copies of fashion magazines with dress styles, and several pages that were ripped from other magazines that showed clothing that would appeal to us. My school uniforms were easy, the same style pleated skirt every year and the same type of blouse. I would have preferred to have my skirt sewn a few inches shorter, above my knee, since it was the seventies and all my friends were wearing mini-skirts, but Sister Enid insisted that the hem should fall no shorter than the middle of my knee. I did roll up my waistband to raise the hemline when I was out of Sister Enid's sight, but this did not lend for a neat appearance.

For my other dresses Meera would have me pick out a pattern from one of her books. I would have to take that book home for Sister Enid to approve of my choice before Meera could begin sewing. It was seldom that I returned to have my first choice sewn. Sister Enid would examine the pattern I chose and then browse the book to find one that she felt was more suitable.

Meera took an infinity to measure and consult her clients about the pattern of dress they wanted and if the material was enough, and would they like some buttons here because she had some lovely ones that would give the dress that extra something. Mostly what Meera wanted however, was to talk about her life, about how she was doomed to live forever in her shop earning money to support her dreadful mother. Often, we would see her mother about and knew she could hear but Meera did not care. Her father had passed away some years before, and Meera shared the home with her mother and two younger sisters.

The usual case was that customers would visit their seamstresses and pour out their hearts to them even divulging their closely held secrets. Seamstresses were known to know the stories of all their clients. Maybe Meera did listen to some of her clients, but since I had no story to tell, she told me hers.

Meera had wanted to get married and go on to live her own life, but as she told it, her parents made up flimsy excuses to reject every suitor. She shared that her father once said that she could not marry a certain young man because his mother cooked long-water curry and no daughter of his would marry into a family that was too poor to fix a proper meal. Meera knew that his intention was to have her remain single and live at home so that the parents would not lose her income. Her only other option was to elope but Meera was not strong willed enough to risk this.

Meera's sister suffered a similar fate. She did not sew and bring in an income, but she took care of the household chores and tending to the needs and wishes of her parents. She also was too valuable to the parents for them to let her go. Both women resented the fact that their brothers were free to get married and take their wives and leave but that they were denied that choice.

Another sister was born when both young women were in their late twenties and already classified as lifelong spinsters. Meera told me that she would not let that sister suffer the same fate and fall into the rut that she and her other sister were in. She said that she would see to it that her sister had the freedom to get married and leave the dismal home.

I hope Meera was able to help her sister.

Chapter 52
Church

One of the habits that was established soon after we settled in Port Mourant, was attending church services on Sunday mornings. We attended St. Joseph's Anglican Church which sat next to St. Joseph's Anglican Primary School. Mass started at 7:00am, but the more devout could attend matins which began at 6:30. We attended mass. We could not eat before mass. I am not sure where this rule came from but I think I may have paid better attention if I did not have to mind the rumblings of my stomach.

It seemed to me that, even though the attendees might have been good Christians and prayer was their number one reason for attending church, there was a second agenda at play in many cases. First there was the bevy of beautiful sisters who came to church dressed to the nines in perfectly coordinated outfits. They were all talented with a sewing machine so they were able to sew matching hats, bags and dresses to complement their shoes. They did not just walk to church, they paraded to church. Many thought their agenda was to "run race" to see who could dress "more fancy" but for me they were a welcome colorful sight.

The altar boys, in their red and white outfits, used their "men in uniform" status to impress the young ladies. Their position in the front of the church afforded then a good view of the congregation so they were able to check out the pretty girls discreetly.

There was another social aspect to church that served the neighborhood young men well. The two local cinemas, Apollo and Roopmahal, would introduce new movies on Sunday evenings: the boys liked to go together so they could discuss the highlights of the movie later, and egg on the hero during the show. There were whispered exchanges as to which theatre hall had the best movie and where they would all go. When there was a dispute as to whether Apollo or Roopmahal had the best show, the young men would lose sight of the fact that they were in church and forget to whisper. The parishioners would have to shush them and remind them of where they were.

I noticed a separation of churchgoers as far as seating was concerned. Most attendees would walk in and take the nearest available seat or any random one. It was not so with the two families that occupied the first two pews on either side of the main aisle. They sat in the same pews every Sunday and no one else sat there even when these families were absent. I was not fully aware that there was some sort of unspoken rule that granted these families a monopoly over those seats until our first Good Friday at St. Joseph's. I could not find a seat anywhere else in the packed church. I noticed a space in the pews of one of the families and made my way there. They seemed surprised at my approach but were pleasant and quickly shifted to make room for me. After church that day I was scolded for going to that pew and was told not to do it again. No explanation was given. Was this some kind of status divide that was not clearly spoken of but everyone (but me) was aware of and observed? Maybe. The two families were prominent in the town so that made sense. And after all, we still sang the stanza in the hymn *All things Bright and beautiful* that stated, "…the rich man in his castle, the poor man at his gate, God made them high or lowly, and ordered their estate."

The best part about Sunday was breakfast after services. On Sundays we got to have "shop bread" instead of the homemade roti we enjoyed during the week. This was special; the loaf was sliced, buttered, toasted on the *tawa* or griddle and served with scrambled eggs, and Vienna sausages sauteed with onions and tomatoes. Delicious!

Chapter 53
Mr. Ramphal

Soon after we started attending church, we had a regular visitor every Sunday after service. Mr. Ramphal was a fixture at church and I don't think he ever missed a service. We were one of the few people who called him Mr. Ramphal and that is because Brother Edward instructed us to do so. Everyone else called him Madman. The one time I forgot and called him Madman Brother Edward gave me a severe reprimand.

As the story goes, Mr. Ramphal was a brilliant young man who received a full scholarship to study at university in England. He left Guyana and started attending school but then he slowly started to deteriorate. One theory suggests that, although most of his expenses were covered, he did not have enough money for food and no one to supplement his funds. Others say that he was terribly lonely and could not concentrate on his studies. Some say rejection by a young lady broke his spirit. His performance in school declined and signs of mental illness became obvious so Mr. Ramphal was sent back to Guyana. Perhaps he had the genes for mental illness but something must have triggered a decline in his mental health when Mr. Ramphal was in England.

Mr. Ramphal always carried a small brown leather suitcase with him and he never let it out of his sight. The contents of the suitcase invited a lot of speculation; was it money, books, important documents? Who knew.

Without warning Mr. Ramphal arrived at our home after church one day. He asked to be let in and Brother Edward seated him at the dining table. He requested a glass of sherry and to speak to the eldest son in the family. His wishes were granted. He declined offers of food or anything else but the sherry.

Paschal, being the eldest son was summoned. Mr. Ramphal invited him to sit in the chair next to him and asked for paper and a pen. He then proceeded to "teach" Paschal. Whatever he said was incoherent, and whatever he wrote was undecipherable, but Paschal was a trooper and sat through the lesson. This usually lasted for an hour or more. After that, around noon, Mr. Ramphal would take his leave. He would then visit my aunt, Mrs. R.N. Persaud, who lived a five-minute walk from our house, where he would have lunch. My aunt said he would have lunch then sit in silence for a long while before leaving. This became a routine every Sunday and at the time no one seemed to think of it as being strange.

A number of years later a hit and run driver struck Mr. Ramphal and he died by the roadside. The lock on his suitcase broke with the impact to reveal sheets of paper with scribbles and numbers that defied understanding. To us it appeared as nonsense but to Mr. Ramphal that must have been his life's work, his manifesto, or a solution to a problem of great import.

Chapter 54
Cleaning Up

A thorough cleaning of house and yard was carried out before the holidays, or when we were expecting visitors from abroad who were treated as royalty. I received the same treatment when I returned for a visit leading my nephew Joshua, who still lived in Guyana at the time, to ask "so who is coming, Queen Mary, that I have to do all this?"

Sister Enid, with the help of young women in the area, would wash the walls of the house to get rid of the red dust that would settle there, they would scrape the wooden stairs with a scraper so that the wood grain would be visible, the kitchen cupboards would be cleaned out, and everything from the pantry would be removed until it was scrubbed and dry.

Brother Edward would be in charge of taking care of the yard. He would hire help and pay a fair price, yet at the end of each day he would give a little extra in the form of a shot or two of rum, conversation, and a hot dinner. This resulted in the job taking many more days than expected. I have a feeling that this was exactly what Brother Edward expected and wanted to happen even though others thought he was being taken advantage of. He had grown up poor and perhaps saw this as a way to give back, however small. Every workman who ever helped us received the same treatment.

Chapter 55
Christmas in Port Mourant

Our first Christmas in the new home in Port Mourant was different from those we spent while on holiday from Orealla. We now had a Christmas tree, a five-foot skinny fake fir that stood in a corner of the living room. We decorated it with stretched out cotton wool snow, shiny balls and tinsel and garlands, but there were never any wrapped presents under it. In our area the only time a present would be wrapped would be for a wedding and even then, not everyone bothered to do this. A birthday was not an occasion to receive presents; a special meal, usually chicken curry, and a trip to the movies were more common.

When we stayed at the Ajees' home over the holidays there was no stove or oven so the traditional Christmas cakes, fruit cake and pound cake (which we called sponge cake) had to be taken to Joe Gomes bakery to be baked. Mr. Joe Gomes (Juggums as everyone called him) would bake pans of cake for a fee depending on the size of the pan, and the sizes were not standard. His bakery was in high demand on Christmas and New Year's.

Early in the morning a day or two before the actual holiday Mr. Gomes would heat up his ovens and take the pans of batter as they came in. They early birds were able to get theirs baked quickly, but Sister Enid liked to wait after a few batches were baked so that the oven would be primed. Often two of us children would be sent to hold a place in line, which grew longer as the day progressed; when we were soon to be called up one of us would run home and give the word. The ladies would then fill the baking pans with batter and hurry down to the bakery.

Very few of the baking pans we used then were store bought. Cut off cans that previously held Golden Cream margarine, or ghee or Edger Boy biscuits were used and they worked just fine.

This year there was no need to line up at Juggums bakery for Sister Enid now had her Falks stove and oven that she brought from Orealla, along with her store-bought baking pans. Sister Enid was an expert at using the kerosene stove and oven which could be temperamental, and her cakes were always exceptional.

On Christmas morning I would take around a basket in our neighborhood and distribute slices of cake that Sister Enid had carefully wrapped, to our neighbors who were not Christian. During their special holidays they would share traditional sweets or gifts with us also; mithai and other delicacies from our Hindu neighbors, and vermicelli cake or a chunk of meat from our Muslim friends.

Sister Enid promised she would try her hand at black cake the next Christmas and she kept her word. By then she had a gas cooker with a built-in oven; previously she had to place her oven on top of the stove. Her black cake was a resounding success.

Black cake has its origins in the English plum pudding. It is a dense fruit cake made with macerated raisins, prunes, maraschino cherries, currants and citron, lots of eggs, sugar, and not much flour. The ground-up fruit is soaked in port wine for months before being baked into a black cake. After the cake is baked it is sprinkled lavishly with rum to keep it moist. The Caribbean spiced up rum version of the traditional plum pudding is much prized in the region for holidays and weddings. For weddings, a layer of icing is added, but I prefer the plain Christmas version.

Another pleasant tradition started that Christmas. Uncle Nelson started sending us a giant Christmas box from England. There was always the biggest tin of Quality Street chocolates, a can of Peak Frean biscuits, apples, grapes and walnuts, and sometimes a bottle of Hennessey's Cognac.

Christmas was the only time we had apples from abroad, usually the Red Delicious variety. This fruit became so closely associated with the holiday that many referred to it as Christmas apple, to differentiate from the local sugar apple, monkey apple or star apple.

Chapter 56
Our Headmaster and Teachers

School was always the constant in our lives and our teachers had a great impact on us.

Our headmaster's contribution to education is renowned in Guyana. The school he founded is now named after him and it still bears a stellar reputation. Students are still inspired by the school's motto, *Per Ardua, ad Astra*, through hard work to the stars.

Despite the tropical heat and humidity, Mr. Chandisingh was always dressed in a suit and tie. The material seemed to be tweed but I cannot be sure. His grey hat, which looked like a fedora, completed his outfit. He rode his bicycle to school every day and set the example for punctuality.

Our dealings with Mr. Chandisingh were infrequent. We heard from him if he chanced to open our textbook and saw the stamp of any store instead of the school stamp. Students were supposed to buy their textbooks from the office unless your parent or a close relative sold books. I was confronted once for having an alien stamp, and although my book came from our uncle's bookstore, I did not have the same last name. I was too intimidated by Mr. C's presence to offer a defense so I simply bowed my head as he scolded me.

My closest encounter with Mr. Chandisingh came in fifth form. We needed a substitute for English Class and Mr. C. volunteered. English was his specialty.

The first thing he did was write a sentence on the blackboard: *Walking along the road, I saw three dead men lying on the grass.* It was his famous dangling participle sentence. He would tell us all about dangling participles, then give us further examples, or ask us to give examples. It was a stressful hour for we were on edge hoping he would not call on us. Mr. C. substituted for our English teacher about three times during fifth form. Each time he taught the same lesson using the same sentence. It must have been his favorite.

In recognition of his dedication to pioneering secondary education in the Corentyne/Berbice area of Guyana Mr. J.C. Chandisingh was awarded the MBE by Her Majesty, Queen Elizabeth II.

Most of our teachers had not gone to four-year colleges or beyond, and had not earned degrees in the subjects they taught. Some had completed training at the Teacher's Training College in Georgetown, many became great teachers through experience, and many were freshly minted high school graduates who had done well and were deemed qualified to pass on what they had learned.

Whatever the background of our teachers, their dedication to their profession and their students were key to our success. That, and they had the total support of our parents. There was no question that a parent would take the side of a teacher in any conflict that arose, for what reason would a teacher have to see a student fail when their success is reflected in that of their charges?

One of the more memorable teachers we had was a gentleman who declared himself a "piece of mathematical dynamite" in jest. He must have been so for he helped me understand the jargon of Algebra, at least for me to remember it long enough to pass the subject in GCE. Mr. Dynamite was a stickler for students paying attention; if they did not, a quick slap at the back of the head with the Algebra or Geometry book would bring them back to the present and to what he was saying. And those were hefty tomes.

Mr. P is another teacher whom I recall fondly. He taught French, was hard of hearing, and was very enthusiastic in his delivery. We could hear him across several classrooms and he led his class in conjugations or declinations or verbs and nouns. I learned the conjugation of *avoir* just by listening the rhythmic *j'ai, tu as, il a, elle a* etc. as Mr. P recited the words in time to the slapping of his shoe on the wooden floorboards of his classroom.

Another memorable teacher was one we secretly referred to as the missing link. We were in third form and were learning about evolution when one day this massive individual appeared in our classroom to substitute for one of our regular teachers who was on extended leave. Mr. Substitute was well over six feet tall, had shoulder length hair, spoke with a gruff voice that made his prominent Adam's apple bob up and down, and he walked with a pronounced stoop.

We were in awe of this teacher and once he entered our classroom, silence ruled. But as soon as he was gone the room became abuzz with what must have happened to him. Comic books were widely popular and the theories varied from radiation to someone putting a curse on his mother before he was born. I am not sure who came up with the name, but *missing link* stuck.

Whatever we thought of the appearance of our substitute teacher he did his job effectively.

Chapter 57
August Vacation

I was not a fan of the long August holiday that lasted from mid-June to late August, nor of weekends and holidays. I liked school, for there I had a social life. I had friends to speak with, and talk about books, and gossip and share dreams. At home the boys and Brother Edward would be out and about so there would be just me, Sister Enid and the young woman helping us. There was housework of course. Although I did not do as much as my neighbors, I still had to do my share of chores. I did not mind chores like bringing in the laundry and folding, sorting, and putting it away, or even washing dishes, but dusting and sweeping sent me into sneezing fits.

My favorite chore was "picking rice". This meant picking out the kernels that were black or discolored. We bought rice in bulk; this came in a hundred-pound jute sack so we were never out of rice to pick. The picked rice would then be transferred to an empty Edger Boy biscuit tin, ready for cooking. The mindless task of picking rice allowed me to dream. I dreamt of places I read about or of solving mysteries worldwide like the children in the Enid Blyton mysteries. My favorite daydream, however was to plan my cozy home inside of a huge hollowed out tree trunk. There was a place to sleep, shelves with books, dishes, pots and pans, and clothes in a cardboard box. A white bucket full of boiled water for cooking and drinking sat by a wash-up area, and a small pile of wood sat beside the door. Cooking would be done outside and from witnessing Sister Enid's experience with burning wet wood in the fireside in Orealla, I knew the importance of having dry wood to start a fire, hence the wood inside. I was never able to realize the dream of a tree trunk home, but I do love the conveniences of a modern home with push-button appliances.

For a great part of the summer my nephews would help Uncle Richard in the bookstore. The booklists for all the schools in the areas that the bookstore served would be collected, the books ordered, and then they had to be unpacked, sorted, stamped, and shelved. The busiest time however was August when everyone came in to fill their school book requirements. The boys enjoyed working in the bookshop and that kept them busy over the break. That and going to the cinema and playing cards with their friends.

I had unlimited novels to occupy me, but eavesdropping on Sister Enid and our helper as they gossiped, especially when doing laundry, was even better entertainment. From them I learned who "tek up wid who" and were living together without being married, and which woman rushed into the house of her husband's mistress while he was there and dragged him out, and which boy tricked a family saying he was going to marry their daughter but then went for the match with the bigger dowry. Often, I barely knew any of these people but their stories were riveting.

About four times over the vacation weeks Sister Enid and I and our neighbors would go to the movies. The big hits were usually timed to be released at Apollo and Roopmahal cinemas over the August holiday weekend. Both cinemas were walking distance from our house. Matinee shows were common but going to the 8:00pm show was more of a special occasion. One had to go very early to secure a seat when the hits first opened, or be disappointed if the show was sold out and one had to return home and feel "like you dressed ninety-nine for nothing."

On occasion over the break, I would accompany Sister Enid to the market. Port Mourant Market was a treat for the senses. The colorful displays of fruit and vegetables included royal purple bigan or eggplant, mangoes from yellow to cherry red, every shade of green in produce, and the silvery tone that dominated the fish and shrimp area.

The clothing of the women rivaled that of the products. Dresses in every hue and pattern shimmied about from stall to stall, and when the women arrived or left the market, a rainbow array of parasols bobbed up and down the road. Those who did not use parasols wore ribboned straw hats or the many-hued plaid of the traditional Madras head covering, the rumal.

The sounds of vendors calling out their wares, '…come buy, nice chokha bigan' or 'young squash, jes pick" and the haggling over prices lent its music to the scene. The rough skins of pineapple and breadfruit and scaled fish contrasted with the silky smoothness of eggplant, squash, or fish with no scales. The coolness near the crush-ice stand tempered the tropical heat, and the wafting smells lead one to either the syrupy sweetness of the julab juman and jalebi stand or to the fish vending spot.

Sister Enid usually bought a lot of most items because she had a large family to feed. I would watch her skillfully bargain with the vendors over price, or suggest that having bought so much would the seller toss in some more beans at no extra cost. She was often disappointed that the sellers would not let her break the tips of okra to see whether they were young and fresh, or old and hard; if the tips snapped cleanly and easily, that meant young and tender and fresh. Sister Enid was at her best at the fish stand. She taught me the rules about purchasing the freshest fish; the eyes have to be bright, bright, the flesh should be transparent and should bounce back when you poked it, and the blood should be bright red. She looked for these attributes whenever she purchased fish.

I failed miserably the one time I was sent to market when Sister Enid was busy. I went to the fish stand and was examining the fish to make sure it would pass muster with her. I may have stood a tad too long staring at the fish for the seller soon slammed her hatched on the board and demanded to know whether I was "go jus stan-up deh like you stuppid and block me stall, or you go buy?" I bought. The fish did not pass Sister Enid's test and I turned to leave but again she slammed the hatched and wanted to know why I was "turning you face, what wrong with de fish? Dis a fresh, fresh fish." Now she was waving the hatchet at me. When she raised her head and I saw the face under the wide brim of the straw hat I realized that I was speaking to the dreaded Auntie I. The fish women were known for their loud and brash behavior, and for their use of colorful language, but Auntie I's reputation for carrying these to the extreme was legendary. I was too intimidated to tell this woman, who was proficient with the hatchet that she used to punctuate her words, that I did not think the fish was fresh enough so I bought a small piece.

I was never sent to market on my own again for it was decided that I did not know how to "buy" and I was ok with that. Not knowing how to buy was listed among the things that "girls nowadays do not know how to do", for girls nowadays did not have *sahoor* to do work. When Sister Enid was twelve, she could cook and clean and wash and take care of a house, but girls nowadays just wanted to shine up their skin and read love book.

The best stalls for us children were those with the julab jamun and jalebi and other desserts, the one with syrupy crushed ice, and the pastry cart, all of which I could visit on my own, but Sister Enid always bought a host of these anyway. On a hot day nothing hit the spot like crushed ice. Even though we all called it "crush ice" it was really shaved ice created by using a metal shaver to shave a huge block of ice. Sister Enid would take a pitcher and have it filled with the crushed ice and red syrup. If we had a penny and no container, we could still get an ice ball where the shaved ice would be squashed into a ball and then covered in red syrup. We ended up with a happy stomach and sticky hands and feet.

My very favorite activity during the holidays and weekends was when we would all be home in the evenings and would play games after dinner. We played *trump charl*, a popular card game in Guyana, Ludo, Snakes and Ladders, checkers, and chess. The card game was more popular for many could play at once. When our board game pieces were lost, we would substitute buttons, and when the boards became worn and ratty we made new ones out of cardboard and colored pencils. These worked fine until we received new ones.

Chapter 58
Auntie Rana

One of Sister Enid's most interesting and entertaining friends was Auntie Rana. I loved the way she spoke for she always had a proverb or an analogy to explain everything.

If Sister Enid would relate an incident where someone was mean to her, Auntie Rana would comfort her with phrases like, "Sister Enid, when people don't like you, they does give you basket to fetch water, but you know you don't have to take none basket from dem because you gat you own good, good bucket. And nah one bucket, look how much good, good bucket you gat"

Once Sister Enid was miffed because she asked a neighbor to lend her some garden tool or other and they refused, even though they were always borrowing her things and this was the first time she had asked them to loan her anything. Auntie Rana consoled her with, "Sister Enid, don worry, is not one hand does clap, next time they come knocking on you door to borrow anything you know what you got to do."

There was a time when prominent people were switching parties to reap benefits from the one in power. Auntie Rana's summation of this betrayal was "even them who think they big shot and that they better than me and you, running to set they mouth where soup a leak."

Upon hearing that someone was deeply hurt by gossip that was not true, Auntie Rana was prompted to declare that, "Sister Enid, tongue na gat teeth but it can bite hard, and one day somebody going to set they tongue on dem same people who shredding other people like that, you wait and see."

Auntie Rana's sister-in-law was due to visit soon. There seemed to be some competition between these ladies who were married to two brothers. The sister-in-law especially seemed to like to laud her possessions over Auntie Rana. She would be sure to point out her new dress and how much per yard the material cost and how she was lucky to find these nice shoes at the Bata store and so on. This time Auntie Rana had just had a lovely dress sewn and new shoes to go with it. She was thinking of showing off these items if Shira started up with "her nonsense." Auntie Rana said that she hoped Shira would be humble this time so that she won't be tempted to bring out her finery for "when eye nah see, heart nah burn" and she did not want to have Shira covet her things and put bad eye on them.

Upon hearing that two young women who could not stand each other previously had married two brothers and were now friends, probably because they now shared the same home with a termagant of a mother-in-law who favored neither woman, Auntie Rana's comment was, "Sister Enid, when thunder roll, cat and dog come buddy-buddy."

One day Sister Enid told Auntie Rana that she wanted to go see a particular movie that was very popular but that a friend who saw it said it was no good and not worth the dollar. Auntie Rana's response was, "Sister Enid, nah tek you mattie eye fo see, go see am fo yourself."

Sister Enid had some quirky phrases herself. If she would be talking about someone and they stopped by soon after she would declare that "they would live long for she just called their name", or if a spoon would fall that meant that visitors were coming, or if she spoke someone's name and she sneezed right after that, it meant that everything she said about them was the "tru, tru God truth". These days, if my left palm should itch, I would wonder about all the possible ways I could come into a bit of money for, according to Sister Enid, an itchy left palm meant that one would receive money; if the right palm itched then money would be lost. Also, if one's right eye would "jump", or have a spasm, that meant something bad would happen, but the left eye jumping would have the opposite effect.

I even use, or at least think about, some of the sayings from these two women when the appropriate situation arises.

Chapter 59
Words

In high school I struggled to find my identity. I was not in the camp of those who were known as "nice gyal" or pretty girls. I did not have flair or charm, or proficiency in any sport; in fact, I was very uncoordinated physically. To make matters worse, I became more conscious of my birthmark. The birthmark did not matter much in elementary school but now, with the onset of puberty, I became more focused on my appearance and the mark brought my spirits down considerably. This may have been depression but we did not speak of those things then.

The one consistent thread of positivity during that time was my way with words. I read a lot, thanks to Uncle Richard, who generously let us read the books from his bookstore, R. H. Makhanlall Bookshop, the most widely known one in the Berbice area. I read anything I could get my hands on, from Enid Blyton mysteries when I was younger to Ian Fleming, Allistair McClean, Agatha Christie, the classics etc. The only kind of books I was not allowed to read were the Mills and Boon novels, (Harlequin Romances in the USA), that all my friends were reading. Sister Enid felt that I would get ideas of boyfriends and romance and such and that was not a good thing in her book. I still read them though. There was an unofficial club at school where five or six girls would each purchase a different romance novel and swap with each other. I did not have one to swap but they let me read theirs anyway before school started, and during lunch if I hurried back in time. If I needed to finish a book so that someone else could get it, I would take it home and read it by flashlight under the covers. As a side note, I did get away with reading *The Godfather* at home and was in disbelief that Sister Enid did not ban me from reading it, given the explicit scenes that peppered its pages. It later occurred to me that she thought it was a book about religion, given the title and the appearance of a cross-like object (puppet controls) on the cover.

I became used to being among the last to be picked for any sports team, but was usually the first or second to be chosen for debate. My cousin, Dushant, was often chosen before me if he was there. I was also proud of the number of times I was called upon to read my essay before the class. This was a common practice and an honor if one wrote a particularly good essay, and the number of times I was chosen filled me with confidence. I had found my niche, my strength: words. Later, when I applied to college in the U.S.A. and put English ass my desired major, Brother Edward made me change it. His reasoning was that if one wanted to make it in America, they should study science or maths. I was not a strong maths student but I did well in science though not as well as I did in English, so I listed my major as Biology.

I would have been proud to say that I used words only to bolster my self-esteem, or to excel in school, but I did not. I also used words as a self-defense tool. That would have been all right if I made my point and moved on, but there were times when I used words to hurt others, especially when any negative reference to my appearance was made. I am not proud of those moments.

Chapter 60
Discipline

In primary school discipline was meted out with store-bought English-style wild canes, whips cut from nearby trees, or wooden rulers. For minor offences the errant child would be made to stand in front of the class throughout the lesson in full gaze of classmates, and even those from other classes so that everyone would be aware that they had committed a wrong. No punishment was carried out in private. This increased exposure made the chances of a parent finding out one was in trouble even greater, for at least one student would be sure to tell the tale to a parent who would then feel compelled to inform the parents of the perpetrator. That meant double the punishment, for parents always believed that the teacher was right and they would often supplement with at least a good talking-to, and increased scrutiny of one's school work and studies.

There was no caning in high school as I remember. If a student misbehaved a note would be sent to the parents giving details of the wrong that their child did, or they would be invited to school to discuss the matter with the principal. It was rare that we saw parents visit with the principal.

Formal caning or lashing was only carried out in homes for serious offences. Parents, especially mothers, believed in lecturing or threats. Often the fathers would be at work and a harried mother juggling cooking, cleaning, washing, and the care of numerous children did not have the time to investigate every instance of who first started an argument or of who was the first to hit; her response to one calling her attention to a fight would be "… if you make me come deh I will bust all two ayu head", or …"you ah talk back to me, nah make me come deh or me go haul out you tongue". When neighborhood kids would raid the trees for mangoes or guavas, many a mother would respond with, "... if me ketch you me go chop out you hand, then me go see how you go thief." Often the thieves would be back in a couple of days.

The demonic yet empty threats would certainly have led to children being taken away from their families, and mothers being punished in other countries, but in Guyana they were ignored by all. Even though no mother ever carried out these threats, the fact that she uttered them would lead children to cease fighting. They now knew that mother was getting angry and the next step would be for her to come and give a few good heavy-handed claps to the bottom, or cuffs of the upper arm, or the painful twitching of one's ear for being "hard ears ", and not listening to her and following her directions.

One did not have to hide any errant behavior from just parents. For us, it was truly a scenario where the village raised the child. Anyone who saw a child misbehaving had the parents full support to admonish that child or report the behavior to the parents. On one occasion a concerned gentleman thought he saw one of my nephews gambling under a tree. He came to the house and reported this to Brother Edward. When asked which one of the boys was the culprit, he said it was the one with glasses. Brother Edward had all five boys stand in police line-up fashion in front of the gentleman. Three of the five boys wore glasses at the time and that stumped him, but Brother Edward thanked him and assured him that he did the right thing. If any of the boys were indeed gambling that day, his identity still remains a mystery.

I imagine most, if not all of us Guyanese children, received similar treatment both at school and at home but most of us turned out alright as far as I can tell.

Chapter 61
My Nemesis

At one time Sister Enid raised chickens. They were all different and colorful. One was supposed to be an Andalusia Gray and I did like that one best because of its speckled gray and white coloring which was enhanced by its bright red comb. There was also a striking rooster, much like the one on my favorite rooster plate; he had shiny red-brown feathers and a brilliant emerald tail.

One of these birds struck me with its puzzling behavior. It was a brown and white hen who would climb the stairs every day, find a box of clean rags that was in the storage room, sit there and lay an egg. Then it would make its way downstairs again. This occurred around the same time every day. How that chicken, whose kind were supposed to be dumb, knew to do this was beyond my comprehension. How she found the box in the first place and then remembered where it was day after day is still a mystery to me.

At some point this batch of chickens were all gone, either sold or eaten. I believe raising chickens stopped after the incident with one of the dinner selections. Rosa was butchering it in the yard for dinner and somehow the body without the head struggled loose from Rosa's hands and started running around. I came out to see what the commotion was all about and saw the headless bird painting the fence, the grass and the white walls of the lower room with the blood gushing from its neck. I disappeared back into the house not waiting to see that chicken run until it dropped dead. A number of years later Sister Enid procured another batch. These were white chickens, a rather dull lot compared to the vibrant set we had before. Even the rooster was white, but unlike his better, more colorful counterpart, he was mean and he hated me. The feeling was mutual.

The rooster, who became known as Dirty Joe because he would get his feathers all covered with dust, was known for pecking others. Most of the folks around would shoo him away with a broom or whatever was at hand and he behaved himself. He tried intimidating the milk lady who came each day gliding regally down the street with her milk can balanced on a coil of cloth on her head. A few loud bangs on the can made Dirty Joe hurry away, and after a few days he did not fly at her anymore. But he must have sensed the fear in me.

Dirty Joe took it upon himself to rush to the front gate every time I came home from school. He would lower his right wing and do what I called a war dance in front of me, staring at me with his evil, beady eyes. I tried using my hat to ward him off a few times but he was not deterred, he just flew at me in a rage. To avoid that I would just stand by the gate and call out so that whatever brave soul heard me would come and drive the demon rooster away.

Dirty Joe knew exactly how to intimidate small children and me, but he was not so smart when it came to fighting the rooster in the pane of glass that stood downstairs. Dirty Joe might have pecked at his reflection forever, even to death, if someone had not removed the glass. It certainly was not me.

One night, thieves came and emptied the cage downstairs of all the hens. Sometimes when we would hear a noise downstairs in the night Brother Edward would first pull on a pair of pants, and stomp about and shout "hold him there" as he took his time getting out the door. His idea was surely to alert the thieves so that they would make their escape before he came downstairs and he would not have to confront them. This usually worked in those days, but not when living conditions deteriorated and people became desperate.

Dirty Joe was sold, to my relief and delight, and that was the last time Sister Enid kept chickens.

Chapter 62
Banned Goods

Petty burglary was nothing new, but instances of thievery increased as conditions became worse in the country. We were waiting for the better lifestyle that gaining independence promised but the opposite occurred. Spraying to control the mosquito population was halted, the regular dredging and cleaning out of the drainage trenches was also stopped, but worst of all the imported foods that had become a vital part of our diet were banned.

Irish potatoes, as we called them regardless of their country of origin, were no longer available, at least not legally. No curry or stew we made was complete without the addition of potatoes. Canned sardines, salmon, and corned mutton, which we relied on when fish was scarce to improvise a quick meal were also no longer imported. Wheat flour, another vital part of our diet, though not banned became available in limited quantities, and the lines for kerosene were impossibly long, with supplies running out before everyone could get what they needed. Some items we could replace with locally grown produce and this is what the government urged us to do, but for many there was no substitute, they had become an integral part of our diet.

The shortages lead to smuggling across the Corentyne river between Nickerie on the Suriname side, and Skeldon. There were laws established to deter smuggling. Not only were the smugglers to be punished, but those who were caught in the possession of banned goods were threatened with fines or jail time. These laws and threats did not end smuggling. Despite the danger of being caught and punished, the practice continued. As we heard it, some of the policemen who were assigned to control the illegal entry of banned items from Nickerie were in the same situation as the rest of us and would turn a blind eye in exchange for some of the said goods or cash.

Brother Maywah and Sister Marge still lived in Skeldon and they would secure items that they knew we could use. Sister Enid would then travel to Skeldon and pick these up. The car ride back to Port Mourant was nerve wracking as Sister Enid told it, for one was always on the lookout for policemen who would make random searches of cars or buses coming from the direction of Skeldon. One also had to be careful of the taxi driver for the rumor was that some were in cahoots with the policemen and they would all share in the goods that were seized. Although those in possession would lose their stash of goods if caught, I've never heard of anyone being fined or thrown in jail for possession of banned items. Thankfully, the car in which Sister Enid was riding was never stopped.

Even the products that were made in Guyana became difficult to obtain. The margarine that we relied on for so long was unavailable because of production issues. The government must have considered this a necessary item for margarine was legally imported from Trinidad. It came in dainty little plastic tubs with floral designs. This was new to us for the Golden Cream margarine we had before only came in tins.

Over time, as shortages increased and living conditions became less tolerable, burglaries increased and thieves became bolder. Simple theft eventually escalated to robbers entering homes with cutlasses demanding jewelry and money. Residents eventually resorted to dividing their jewelry and money into two bundles, one for the thieves and one to keep. It was not long before the thieves figured this out so they began to demand two stashes of jewelry and cash. People now lived in fear of being attacked and windows and doors became boarded up. As Sister Enid put it everyone slept "with one eye open."

Chapter 63
Folklore and Superstitions

I woke up one morning with a bruise on my arm. Rosa saw it and right away declared that I had been sucked by a firerass. A firerass, also known as Old Haig, was an evil woman who had the ability to appear as an ordinary human being during the day but when she needed her drink of rejuvenating blood, she sheds her skin in the dead of night, turns into a fireball, and flies to the house of her targeted victim. The old Haig is supposed to favor the fresh blood of newborns, and would often be blamed if a baby died and showed a bluish hue, but usually an Old Haig would settle for any other victim.

It did occur to me that I was rather small and skinny and would not be the prime target for a blood sucker of any kind, except mosquitoes. If I was an Old Haig, I would not have chosen me for a blood feast, considering the other juicy candidates that were everywhere. Maybe my blood was tastier. I did love sweets. But what did I know? It did scare me however that a wild, evil woman was able to enter a secured home and suck my blood without anyone knowing it. And here I was, thinking that the bruise came from hitting my arm at the side of the kitchen counter the day before.

Jumbie was another being that filled us with fear. A jumbie was the evil spirit of one who was dead, mainly one who did not die a peaceful death, but was suddenly and violently taken from this earth and was now back to seek revenge. I suppose anyone who was not nice to someone who had died had reason to fear jumbie, but as I heard it, jumbies did not care whether they struck those who hurt them or not, any random soul would do. That seemed unfair to me. I figured if I was a jumbie I would make sure that those who hurt me suffer to the greatest extent possible for their deeds, but what right would I have to hurt others? Where was the fun in that?

What a jumbie did to its victims was never made clear. All I heard is that if you go out alone at night "jumbie would hold you". What the jumbie did after holding its victims is still a mystery to me.

Backru, or baccu, was another unwelcome spirit. The bakru was not evil but was said to be controlled by evil beings. It was supposed to be a little man who could upend one's life with mischief, maybe like a poltergeist.

The sandcoker tree was feared. This was our local terminology for the silk cotton tree which is common around Guyana. Legend has it that the Dutch who ruled Guyana from the early 1600s to the early 1800s, fearing loss of their treasure if they were overthrown, buried their wealth under a sandcoker tree, then killed the slaves who buried it and drained their blood over the roots so that their spirits could protect it. Very few would chance disturbing a sandcoker tree, and this belief is so strong that there is a specimen along the Mahaica highway that no one would cut down for fear of becoming a victim of the curse on these trees. The government made many attempts to hire contractors to chop down the tree but finally gave up trying after countless unsuccessful attempts, and diverged the road instead.

Besides spirits, there were other practices we were made aware of. We were cautioned not to step over the feet or legs of someone who was sitting in our path for if we did, they would stop growing. This might have been good news for someone who was older and overweight, but not a youth. We also could not sweep the feet of a young lady for then she would never get married. And heaven forbid one should pick up a broom and sweep the house after dusk, for then one would be sweeping away all the barracat, or wealth, of the house.

One of the most feared sounds was to hear the persistent crying of dogs or cats in the night. It was believed that when this happened it heralded the death of someone in close proximity. People would begin to be extra careful to avoid accidents and would look to those who were sickly and wonder if they were next. I have heard from many that this phenomenon was not to be dismissed lightly because it came true often. It is said that animals have a sixth sense to detect the approach of death so there may be some validity in this, but I have no proof.

Chapter 64
Religion

There were/are several major religions in Guyana. The various denominations of Christianity, Hinduism, and Islam are the dominant practices. There are smaller factions like Kali Mai Church and Clap-Hand Church, that are practiced by few.

The Hindus and Muslims who were brought to Guyana as indentured servants from India were able to practice their religion freely, and temples and mosques were erected to fill the need for places of worship. Christian churches were already established by earlier rulers, and the Anglican, Roman Catholic, Lutheran and Presbyterian Churches took charge of the religious and educational needs of the communities they served. The mission schools were free to attend and the Churches footed the expense of educating elementary school children. High School was not free unless one obtained a scholarship.

The freedom to practice one's religion became an issue, however, when prospective teachers applied for teaching positions. Since Christian denominations controlled the schools, it was often a requirement for the applicant to join the Church that governed the school, and most prospective teachers did join. Occasionally a Church would demand that the whole family convert before the young teacher would be hired. Many families complied, and so the number of Christians grew. This did not stop the families from continuing to practice their former religion, however. Hindu or Muslim feast days were still celebrated and traditions associated with those days were still carried out regardless of the Christian status of the family.

One Church that was a hush-hush topic in our house was the Kali Mai Church, especially when Brother Edward was around. This was the main church of those of Madrasi heritage who hailed from the south of India. The religion is a combination of Hindu and Dravidian folk practices and traditions.

I believe that we did not discuss this religion at home because the practice supported the belief of possession by spirits and conducted animal sacrifices and the exorcism of evil entities. I also heard rumors of the drinking of the blood of the sacrificed animals. Although the family does not fully support this religion, a distant relative is known to have sought the help of its priests. As I heard it, this young woman suddenly began speaking in tongues. No one could understand her but some of her words were recognized as being Dutch so she was deemed to be possessed by a Dutch spirit. Visits to western-trained doctors did not help, home remedies did not help, visits from the Christian and Hindu priests did not help, so as a last resort, the family took her to have the spirit exorcised at a Kali Mai puja.

The family was asked to bring a black rooster and certain herbs and spices. Word has it that when the ceremonial drumming began, this young woman got up and began to "play" or dance wildly, pulling at her hair, tossing back her head and rolling her eyes. She danced to the drumming until she collapsed in a sweaty pile. After the sacrificial ceremony, the young girl was sent home with follow up instructions and a warning that she needed to return at the same time every year to keep the supposed persistent spirit away. The woman immediately resumed her natural personality and speech and forgot every bit of Dutch she had spoken before. Although she now lives abroad and is much older this woman has made it her mission to return to Guyana every year to participate in this cleansing puja.

The Jordanites were a mystery. On occasion we would notice tall Black me wearing white robes walk down the street. In unison everyone would cross the street and keep their eyes averted. These actions inspired fear of these people but I did not know what we needed to be afraid of. It was just accepted that Jordanites were not good people and should be avoided.

We lived close to the race course and about once per year we would hear loud singing and clapping. Everyone referred to this as the "clap hand church". The leaders would come from America to lead prayer services. The race course was large enough to accommodate the crowds that gathered and they performed with gusto in their praise of God with loud singing and rhythmic clapping. I am not sure whether this church was Baptist or Pentecostal but their services were high-energy.

Chapter 65
Visitors from Abroad

Very few occurrences brought more excitement to a family than having relatives from abroad pay a visit. From the time the flimsy air mail sheet arrived with the news of the pending visit preparations began.

The house was scrubbed from top to bottom, the mattress where the visitor or visitors would sleep would be refilled to boost comfort, the best pillows and towels would be brought out from the "good" stock in the wardrobe, and arrangements would be made for a car or a bus, depending on how many were interested in going, to take the welcoming party to the airport.

Besides being eager to see relatives whom one had not seen in years, excitement would be generated by the treats and wonderful things that the relatives would usually bring from abroad. And some of the visitors would speak with an accent or use phrases like "that's rad", "far out", or "boy, that's some mango". We stood in awe of those who lived abroad, they were able to see and do things that we only saw in movies or read about in books. We all hoped to follow in their footsteps someday.

When Auntie Ann visited from England a busload of relatives went to greet her at the airport. This was when we were young children and the mass exodus of young people was not yet in full swing so visitors from abroad were infrequent. The group had left Port Mourant early to catch the first crossing of the ferry-boat *Torani*, across the Berbice River (the bridge across this river did not yet exist) just to be sure they would be on time when the plane landed. They arrived in Georgetown during the breakfast hour. The bus unloaded in front of a café and the travelers went in. Once they started speaking the shopkeeper called out to someone in the kitchen, "Freddy", she said, "forget about the boiled eggs, bring out the salt fish, Berbicians in town". Yes, the folks in Georgetown do think that we from Berbice, the country area, are boorish and unsophisticated, but truth to tell I would any day choose a breakfast of salt fish and bake over boiled eggs and toast. The salt fish is a dish is prepared with salted cod where most of the salt is washed out and the fish is then fried in oil and butter with onions and tomatoes. Bake, despite its name is a fried bread, the size of a taco that is served with the salt fish.

The welcoming party then headed to Timehri airport where much hugs and kisses were exchanged with the visitor. There would invariably be a fuss made over who would sit next to Auntie Ann in the bus but everything worked out.

The big event came after the visitor arrived home. Suitcases would be opened and treasures revealed. There was something for everyone, umbrellas that folded, paper fans, delicate handkerchiefs, pot holders, ready-made dresses, Quality Street candies, apples and grapes, and on this occasion, the best cake I have ever tasted. It was orange flavored. The only cakes we had had before were fruit cake, pound cake, and black cake.

When Uncle Nelson visited a few months later there was the same excitement, but Roy seemed quiet and withdrawn. Turns out Uncle Nelson was a dark-complexioned Indian and his complexion remained the same. In Roy's mind, since he was from England, he should not have been dark.

We were taken aback when the visitors from abroad would tell us that they would prefer to have the simple foods they grew up on; the fresh fish and shrimp caught that day, and fruits and vegetables that were picked from the garden just hours before. They would ask for these dishes instead of the meat that was sourced specially for them, chicken, duck or mutton. Everyone thought that they were merely being polite and did not want to burden their relatives with the expense of meat so the families they visited served the best meat they could procure anyway.

I later learned that those who planned to visit relatives in Guyana would prepare for their trip home for months in advance, gathering items that they would take. Everyone would take advantage of sales to stock up. Even if someone was not visiting, they would sometimes ship barrels of goods to their relatives, saving up their sale purchases bit by bit until they had enough for a barrel.

Chapter 66
Medical Practices

An excellent British-trained physician served our community. Dr. Chand hailed from the area and came back home to practice after his graduation from medical school. Port Mourant Hospital was walking distance from us, New Amsterdam Hospital, with more resources, was a half-hour car ride away, and should anyone need more complex care or surgery Georgetown had a plethora of fine doctors, and hospitals.

Despite the availability of these resources many still relied on local treatments for their ailments. One day Sister Enid noticed that my eyes looked yellow. This was confirmed by Rosa, the young lady who helped us with housework. Gandos (jaundice) was the diagnosis. That meant that I had to have a treatment called jharay from the local practitioner.

Rosa accompanied me. The practitioner, a woman, brought a taria (shallow brass dish) and placed it before me, then she brought mustard oil, water, and plucked some grass, The curer then poured the mustard oil and water into the taria and pointed out that even when she rotated the dish the two substances did not mix. Then she bade me put my big toes at the edge of the dish as she stirred the oil and water with the handful of grass. The yellow oil and water appeared to mix and soon a creamy yellow substance filled the taria. The woman told me that that was the gandos coming out of me that made the oil and water mix for how else could oil and water mix?

We had just learned about emulsions and suspensions and solutions in science class so I knew that before long the oil and water would separate again but I did not get a chance to see this happen. The practitioner quickly tossed the contents of the taria, accepted the coins from Rosa and we went our way. It would have been rude for me to say anything so I remained quiet. I did not feel any different and have never had liver issues.

A tummy ache would often be diagnosed as nara by an older person. They were often believed because older folks had lived longer and seen much and thus knew much. The solution was to haul the nara. Someone who claimed to know how to do this would be asked to do the honors. Hauling the nara meant massaging the tummy a certain way to get rid of the pain and whatever was causing it. I hear it often worked but now I wonder if anyone who had serious intestinal issues ever suffered from not receiving proper treatment.

Sometimes babies were diagnosed as having hasli or neck pain. Maybe they slept wrong; many babies were laid in hammocks and I don't know if this contributed to hasli in any way. The cure for hasli was to roll the baby in a bedsheet. Two women would grasp either end of a folded sheet and roll the baby gently back and forth until they were sure the hasli was gone. Many swore by this cure.

Another worry for babies was bad-eye, or the evil eye. To ward this off a black dot would be placed in a prominent position on the baby, usually on the forehead between the eyebrows. If one should pay the baby a compliment saying that the little one was cute or chubby then one had to give the infant a little pinch, for compliments like that could backfire and the infants would suffer the opposite effect. I never understood this but I am careful about complimenting babies just in case. Sometimes the little one would wear a bracelet with black and white beads towards the same end.

If a baby should become fussy after being in the company of others, it would be deemed that someone had given the baby bad-eye. The cure would be to *ouchay* the baby. The smoke from burning garlic and onion skins was said to have powers to clear away the effects of bad-eye.

The ears of girls were commonly pierced when they were still infants. The procedure would involve marking the desired spot of the hole, then poking it through with a larger gauge sewing needle. The needle would be threaded first and the thread would be soaked with hot oil. Then it would be sterilized by fire and cooled before insertion. Part of the thread would be left hanging out of the ears and would be knotted at the ends. Each day the thread would be treated with hot oil and gently pulled through the hole. After about ten days, healing would be complete and "baby" earrings would be inserted. I went through this exact process when I was nineteen. My ears were not pierced when I was a baby but I wanted to wear earrings so one day I marked the spots on my ears and had Rosa do the honors. It did not hurt much. I adhered to the required treatment of hot oil and moving the thread, and before long I was healed. I did not suffer infection at the site and I have not heard of this being common in babies who had their ears pierced and treated this way.

The village dentist was a very stern gentleman and patients, besides being nervous about receiving dental treatment that involved needles and all, were afraid of Dr. Hill. They would often wait until their pain was unbearable before visiting the dentist and the result was usually extraction. I cannot recall anyone having braces in Guyana but most of us have straight teeth. I think enough space was created through extractions for decay that our teeth had enough room to lay out nice and straight.

Another thing I found curious was that, even though visiting the dentist was traumatic for those who needed dental care, many, especially young women, would go to the dentist to have their front teeth "done". This involved drilling into perfectly healthy incisors and placing gold fillings in them. It served as a mark of beauty.

Students who were studying for exams late into the night were given an extra boost of brain power by being served Sanatogen mixed with warm milk by their mothers. It was believed that all that studying could wreak havoc with one's brain if it was not boosted by this nerve tonic so it was required treatment from some mothers.

During one of the most horrific incidents to occur in Guyana much Sanatogen was included in gifts to the grieving families. In 1970, seven men died while cleaning a clarifier tank at the Canje sugar estate. The estate was about a twenty-minute car ride away from Port Mourant but since the men who perished were sugar workers the pain was felt deeply among their fellow sugar factory employees in Port Mourant. A brotherhood existed among sugar workers and so the people of Port Mourant rallied to help their brothers.

As we learned, noxious gases had collected in the clarifier tank overnight, and the valve to release the gases was not opened before the men went in to clean the vessel. One by one they fell unconscious and then died within minutes. Two of the men died as they attempted to carry out their duties at work, the other five perished as they tried to help their friends and coworkers. People flocked to the town to offer sympathy and to help as they could.

It was typical in Guyana that if one noticed any sign of someone being ill or being taken to the doctor or hospital, one is expected to show up and ask questions about the event. The family would willingly fill one in on the details. If one should visit the ill person in the hospital, or when they came home, all of the events and feelings leading up to the illness would be shared. In fact, if one did not show up and ask questions at such an occurrence it would be seen as a mark of disrespect, an indication that one did not care enough to ask about the wellbeing of a neighbor, and one would be chided for it. Medical privacy was not a cause for concern, a neighbor's concern was more prized.

Chapter 67
Shakira Baksh

In 1967, when I was in first form, Miss Shakira Baksh won the Miss Guyana Beauty Contest. She went on to compete in the Miss World pageant in England and was the second runner up. The newspapers loved Miss Baksh, and my friends and I read every bit of information they published on her. The photos were in black and white so we had to imagine the baby-blue sequined dress with the long train that she wore for both contests. A dress that her talented dressmaker-mother sewed.

This in itself was fascinating to us, but it was in 1973, when she and actor Michael Caine married that it showed me that going abroad opened up opportunities that seemed wildly impossible otherwise. 1973 was the year after I graduated high school and was concerned about my future. This was a time of quiet desperation for many young people in Guyana. The future for us in our native land did not seem promising. We reasoned that if it was possible to marry a world class actor, then it could be possible to become a lawyer, or a doctor or scientist, or a host of other exciting things. If only one could leave Guyana and go abroad. Whether to the UK, USA, or Canada, it did not matter.

We could grasp the opportunity to further our studies at The University of Guyana, but the political climate, racial tension, and the requirements for National Service, prevented many young women from East Indian families from attending. Parents were not about to send their young daughters into the hinterland for weeks or months in mixed company to live and work together.

For women the only opportunities were teaching, nursing or working as a bank teller and even those jobs were not guaranteed. It was the same for young men who had a slight advantage of getting civil service jobs. Some of my friends took advantage of offers from hospitals in the UK to become nurses. They were offered room and board and a stipend to use during their years of training, and in return they had to pledge to work at that hospital, at a regular nurses' salary, for a specified length of time. Many started the program with the intention to move on to something else after their obligations were met, but most ended up continuing in nursing. I even considered this for a moment. but I am glad I did not pursue it for nursing did not appeal to me.

Another way to legally move abroad was through marriage to someone who had a green card or citizenship from a foreign country. Many young men who possessed these documents returned to Guyana to choose a bride from the cream of the crop. The women who lived abroad and had their legal papers preferred to find a husband in their adopted country.

Chapter 68
Finding a Bride

Those young men who were fortunate to have their legal papers to reside in another country knew they could have just about any young girl in Guyana that they desired to be their wife. It is said that they came with a list or requirements; light-skin, long hair, and pretty were the top attributes they were looking for. It was well known that the banks usually hired tellers that fit this description so that would be the first stop for these young men.

The prospective grooms usually embellished their circumstances and qualifications. One claimed he was in medical school but was really enrolled in pre-med studies, another dressed in a suit and took his photo in front of an impressive building in Manhattan saying he worked there; he forgot to mention the part about being a janitor, one said he had a car but failed to mention that the fancy sports car he was leaning against was not his. One mother, putting in a good word for her son said that the prospective daughter-in-law would be well taken care of for she would not have to do much housework because in America everything is push-button and her son goes to eat in *roasteraunts* where they will eat roast chicken all the time.

Parents would often go out of their way to have one of these men visit and have a look at their eligible daughter. Having a child abroad was beneficial to the whole family for that child would send gifts, and once they had their papers, they could sponsor their families. Parents would send messages via other relatives saying that they had a young lady available for marriage and would like a prospective groom to visit. Most young men were decent and if they had already found someone (it usually just took a day or two), they would let it be known. Others with less scruples would take the family up on the offer anyway, with the full knowledge that they would not marry that girl. Often, they would bring along a host of friends to the lunch the girl's family prepared knowing that the best would be served, usually curried duck and lots of rum. They would make the rounds and feast heartily, then send their regrets.

The young women in this position were often torn. It was flattering to be shown off to a prospective groom dressed in one's finest, but then they could not be themselves; one had to be the person that the family thought would be most attractive to the young man's parents. Often the instructions were, *put your head down, speak little, smile but don't laugh, answer questions in a soft voice, don't look anyone directly in the eyes, that would be rude, just do as we say.*

Many of these marriages did work out and lasted, but some young women suffered. In one case the young man turned out to be a drunk and accused his wife of only marrying him for his green card for ordinarily a girl like her would spit upon him instead of marry him. He refused to sponsor her saying that she would leave him as soon as she received her papers. The young woman returned home in shame.

Chapter 69
Applying for a Visa

When I graduated from high school, with the help of my brother and sister-in-law in Chicago, I applied to St. Xavier College and was accepted. Brother Homey and his wife Doris, sent all the papers and Brother Edward and I went to the US Embassy to get a visa. I was denied on the grounds that I had the same family connections in the USA as in Guyana; I had siblings in both countries and no stronger ties in Guyana to encourage my return.

I was despondent. I ached to leave Guyana because I did not like the picture of the future that I saw carved out for me if I stayed. I knew I would go through life without ever being able to see the places and do the things I read about. I wanted to get a college education, work at an exciting job, see some of the world, and also get married and have a family. I did not think that dream was unreachable, but every time I was denied a visa my spirits sank even further.

Brother Edward suggested that I attend Berbice High School to sit for the A Level Exams while I waited for a visa. We both thought that I would be granted a visa on the next try.

I had to take a bus to Berbice High School. Duke of York came between 7;00 and 7:30 in the morning and it was packed before it reached my stop. The heat and humidity of all those bodies squashed together in the bus without air conditioning, and often with no hint of a breeze sometimes took its toll. Girls would faint. It might have been the stifling conditions in the bus combined with anemia that caused this.

A curious phenomena occurred among girls who were around eleven and older; they developed a hankering to eat raw rice and would go to great lengths to do this. Sister Enid admitted to filling her dress pockets with raw rice when she was younger and would sometimes chew it in the night. I was one of many who also shared this yearning. We were scolded for doing this for it was thought that our teeth would be damaged, but the urge was too strong to resist.

It turns out that this need for eating raw rice is a form of pica caused by iron deficiency anemia. Many young girls in Guyana did not consume enough iron rich foods to meet the requirements of their bodies. Eating beef was taboo, eggs may have been mainly sold rather than served at home, mutton was consumed once per year during the August holidays, and taking vitamins was not a common practice.

Once Sister Enid learned this, she started me on "building up" in order to boost my health. She consulted the local pharmacist for his recommendation and so I began taking Geritol. I have never fainted.

We applied again for a visa and again I was unsuccessful in receiving one. Each time I was rejected and planned to apply again, another application for admittance to the college had to be made, accompanied by all the required supporting documents. Brother Homey and Sister Doris thankfully handled this end of the visa process but it must have been quite the chore to repeat these steps over and over. Going to Georgetown to apply for the visa was a frustrating process also but Brother Edward knew that I should be in college and he did his best to help.

In the meantime, I had finished my A Level studies and with no visa it was decided that I would teach until I obtained one.

Chapter 70
Teaching

Like the many others who were in my position, I filled the gap while waiting for a visa with a teaching position. I taught at St. Joseph's Anglican School where I had attended primary school. I started by shadowing the Prep A teacher and learned the requirements of the job. I was then given my own Prep B class to teach.

The school had not changed. It was still open concept with the only class dividers being the chalkboards on easels. When I was a student, our classroom was in the upper level of the school where it was markedly quieter compared to the lower floor. The noise level, especially in the Prep A and Prep B areas with twenty-five or more students per class, remained at a constant high because most of the lower classes learned by rote and very few had the required books because their families could not afford them. Spelling words would be written on the blackboard and the entire class would repeat the spelling after the teacher as she pointed out the different letters. Somehow the children managed to learn even with more than one class spelling aloud at the same time. Reading was done the same way. Often the pupils would memorize the words and be able to pretend to read. They would read the words on the board in a sing-song fashion and when asked to read from the book pupils would read "Mother Hen and her chicks went for a walk, but Percy stayed at home", or whatever sentence they learned, in the same manner.

After Prep classes were dismissed, the students from the upper forms would come down to sweep the classrooms. The benches would be placed on the desks and the floor swept clean with homemade coconut brooms.

I learned a sobering lesson during my teaching stint. Often the pupils who lived far away would bring their packed lunches in saucepans. Teachers would supervise lunch time before going on their own lunch break. One day a girl dropped her saucepan and all her food spilled. She began crying uncontrollably even though I told her she could go home to eat and even if she came back late it would be all right.

I did not realize how little I knew of my charges or their home situation until the Prep A teacher whispered in my ear: "How do you know there is more food at home?" I bought a snack from Elfreda, the vendor who sold the most delicious bara and boiled channa in front of the school and gave it to her before I left for home.

I had a hurried lunch and rushed back with food for this pupil. This must be where my need to not waste food originated. I try to always clean my place, and if I leave food, it is because I am just too full or I cannot stomach the food before me. I know that there is some archaic rule that says one should leave a bit of food on one's plate to convey that you have enjoyed the meal and have had enough. It is fine that some subscribe to this bit of etiquette, but I feel no need to do so for my experience with food has been different from theirs.

Chapter 71
Fourth Visit to the U.S. Embassy

I had thought that the third try for a visa would have been a charm but it was not. I was again denied. I began to seriously contemplate joining a nursing program in England. Even though I knew that it was not what I wanted, the need to leave Guyana was strong enough to propel me to contemplate any option.

I continued teaching until I was again called for an interview at the American Embassy. I hoped my fervent prayers would be answered as I stepped before the interviewer for the fourth time. This gentleman hailed from the Chicago area and told me his sister attended St. Xavier's and that it was a tough school. He asked me if I would manage the program in Biology. I said yes. Miraculously, he stamped my passport with a visa to The United States of America.

My calm outward composure was due to the state of shock I was in. I was still in disbelief. The excitement and intense gratitude came later as preparations to leave Guyana began.

As usual, when we visited Georgetown, Brother Edward treated us to an ice cream cone. It was the best ice cream cone I have ever tasted.

***

The new semester at St. Xavier's was to start soon that January and I had less than two weeks to prepare. A flight was booked, I gave notice at my job, packed all necessities and was ready to go.

On January 23, 1977, a carload of us went to the airport, Brother Edward, Sister Enid, Joshua and I. We arrived early (there was never any doubt that we would not). The PanAm plane that was going to take me away to my dreams was already sitting on the tarmac, and then is when it hit me, that withing hours I would no longer be in this land that I prayed so hard to leave. It was a bitter-sweet moment.

The time came for me to board. We said our goodbyes through hugs, kisses and tears. I double checked my hand luggage to make sure that my heaviest piece of clothing was in there. It was a cotton cardigan gifted to me by a relative from abroad. I felt that I was ready for the weather in New York and Chicago.

It was the winter of 1976-1977.

References:

*1   https://guyanachronicle.com/2018/09/16/the-beauty-of-orealla/
*2   https://www.thingsguyana.com/orealla-village-orealla-is-an-arawak-word-which-means-white-chalk/
*3   http://anglicanhistory.org/sa/gy/brett/13.html
*4   https://www.webmd.com/skin-problems-and-treatments/qa/what-are-chiggers
*5   https://www.alamy.com/stock-photo-marabunta-or-spider-wasp-family-pompilidae-solitary-wasp-at-nest-in-41906350.html*1 https://guyanachronicle.com/2018/09/16/the-beauty-of-orealla/
*6   http://chs-jccss.org/blog/murder-on-the-high-seas/comment-page-1/
*7   https://my.clevelandclinic.org/health/diseases/15647-snake-bites/management-and-treatment
*8   https://guyanatimesgy.com/orealla-leading-the-way-in-eco-tourism/
*9   https://dpi.gov.gy/arawak-language-to-be-revived-in-orealla-siparuta/

Related Sites of Interest

https://guyaneseonline.net/2013/01/21/guyanas-fruits-the-awarra-palm-fruit/
https://www.youtube.com/watch?v=hVy3eHFFo0Y
(making hammocks)
https://www.youtube.com/watch?v=TcdyKQp2bkQ
(canoe, matapee)

Acknowledgements

I owe the greatest thanks to my daughters, Nirvana, Karuna and Sarvani; thank you for gracing my life with your presence, and for starting the spark that led me to write this book.

I also thank all those who helped raise me and loved me and added immeasurably to my life after my mother and father were no longer there. Thanks to Sister Pat, Sister Judy, Brother Karanand, Chachi, and Pagli, Sister Enid and Brother Edward, and their sons, my brothers, Paschal, Remi, Roy, Dicky and Joshua, who enriched my life in the past and continue to do so in the present.

Thanks to all those who have encouraged me to write my story over the years, and to those who have read the rough draft and offered invaluable suggestions.

Paschal, Remi, Devikha: your input has made me write a better book.

Jill Janusz Lane: your careful reading, editing and suggestions have improved this book considerably.

Mary Beth Husseini: your encouragement made me plod along and finish what I started years ago.

My Other Book Club friends, Melissa Jacot, Sue Schwartzhoff, Sue Reynolds Acker, Dee Bucur, Brett Singer, Susan Blair: showing interest in my work, reading the rough draft, and asking for more chapters gave me the confidence to continue.

Printed in Great Britain
by Amazon